FRANK LLOYD WRIGHT

FIELD GUIDE

FRANK LLOYD WRIGHT

FIELD GUIDE

HIS 100 GREATEST WORKS

Edited by Marie Clayton

RUNNING PRESS
PHILADELPHIA • LONDON

©2002 Salamander Books Ltd
8 Blenheim Court, Brewery Road
London N7 9NY, United Kingdom

A member of **Chrysalis** Books plc

This edition published in the United States in 2002
by Running Press Book Publishers

9 8 7 6 5 4 3 2 1
Digit on the right indicates the number of this printing

Library of Congress Cataloging-in-Publication 2002100482

ISBN 0-7624-1324-7

Credits
Designed by Mitchell Print and Publishing Solutions
Photographs on pages 2, 220,221,223 & 224 courtesy of
John A. Caulfield
All other photographs Simon Clay/Chrysalis Images
Reproduction: Anorax
Printed in Taiwan

This book may be ordered by mail from the publisher.
Please include $2.50 for postage and handling.
But try your bookstore first!

Running Press Book Publishers
125 South Twenty-second Street
Philadelphia, Pennsylvania 19103-4399

Visit us on the web!
wwwrunningpress.com

CONTENTS

INTRODUCTION

■ ■ ■

"Early in life I had to choose between honest arrogance
and hypocritical humility. I chose the former
and have seen no reason to change."

■ ■ ■

Frank Lloyd Wright is widely regarded as one of the greatest architects of the 20th century. He certainly held this opinion himself: in fact during his lifetime he claimed to be "the greatest architect who ever lived." His contribution to American culture is considered so important that no less than 17 of his buildings have been designated to be retained by the A.I.I. Even apart from this fame as an architect, his life is fascinating - his views were sometimes startling and outrageous and his personal life was complex. Despite the opinion he had of himself as a genius without any faults, he was a spendthrift, a womanizer and designed several buildings with leaking roofs or bulging walls.

Wright's habit of altering the facts to suit himself,

LEFT: *The simple marker at Taliesin West that indicates the final resting place of America's greatest architect. Wright was a complete designer and even the smallest detail did not escape him. His typeface - Eaglefeather - is always associated with him.*

and telling different people different things at different times, means that sorting out the true facts of his life can often be quite difficult. According to official records, he was born on June 8, 1867, in Richland Center, Wisconsin, which was a prosperous market town near Spring Green. In later years he often gave his birthdate as 1869, but that was actually the birth year of his younger sister, Jane. Several Wright family documents and oral tradition both confirm that he was originally called Frank Lincoln Wright. Like many sons born around this period he was probably christened after President Lincoln, who had been assassinated a few years earlier in 1865. His father, William Wright, had been chosen to preside over the ceremony held in Richland Center following Lincoln's death, so it would not have been surprising if he had called his first son after the great president. It is generally believed that his mother renamed the young Frank after her side of the family, following the deterioration of her marriage into open warfare.

Frank's mother, Anna Lloyd Jones, was a teacher, who had been born in Wales in 1839. She had arrived in America with the rest of her large farming family in 1845, and they had all settled in a valley near Spring Green. His father, William Carey Wright was a preacher and musician who had been born in Westfield,

Massachusetts in 1825 where his own father was serving as a Baptist minister. William Wright had studied medicine, but went on to teach music in Utica, New York. He married one of his students, Permelia Holcomb, and they had three children - one of whom died in infancy. William had by now become a preacher and had also been admitted to the bar after studying law. The family moved round and by 1861 had settled in Lone Rock, Wisconsin. However, William found it difficult to make enough money to support his growing family, so to make ends meet Permelia took in boarders. One of these boarders was Anna Lloyd Jones, and after Permelia died in childbirth in 1864, Anna soon set her sights on marrying the 41-year-old widower. For her it was a great match - she was 25 and in danger of becoming an old maid, and William was well educated, composed music and songs and played several instruments. Unfortunately the marriage was never happy - Anna had a terrible temper, which was a symptom of an underlying and serious mental illness.

According to Frank Lloyd Wright, his mother decided he was to be an architect when he was still a tiny baby. She is supposed to have been inspired by the wood engravings of English cathedrals that decorated her young son's nursery. There are several problems with this story - for a start, architecture was not a respected

ABOVE: W.H. Pettit Memorial Chapel (Belvidere, Illinois, 1906).
Adjoining the cemetery, the chapel is a one-story building designed on a
T-plan and constructed of wood surfaced with plaster. It was dedicated to
Dr William Pettit by his wife, Emma, in 1899.

RIGHT: The Frank Lloyd Wright red signature tile that was incorporated
in his buildings from about 1904. Most authorities agree that this new
symbol owes its origins to Japanese prints. In his earlier designs, Wright
had used a Celtic cross.

profession like medicine or law until many years after Frank's birth. Also, since the house where Frank was born was quite small and the three older children from William's first marriage were also living there at first, it is unlikely that there was room for a nursery just for Frank.

Anna was not fond of her stepchildren and often treated them very harshly, so some time after Frank was born they were moved out to live with relatives of their dead mother. In 1869, Frank's sister Jane was born and in 1878 Margaret Ellen, known as Maginel, but Anna made no secret of the fact that Frank was her favorite. Her relationship with William was already deteriorating badly,

11

RIGHT: Francis W. Little House I (Peroria, Illinois, 1902). Originally a brick T-plan house, with a spacious separate stable, the Little House was enlarged in 1909, which elongated its plan. It was such a successful design that it requires very little upkeep.

BELOW RIGHT: The arch of the front door of the Little House is outlined with a wide band of gold-tinted art-glass - the house contains a large amount of beautiful art-glass. Little was a dedicated collector of Japanese prints and Wright later borrowed $10,000 from him to buy the American rights to the Wasmuth Portfolios, offering a selection of his own Japanese prints as collateral for the loan.

OPPOSITE: Henry J. Allen House (Wichita, Kansas, 1917). Wright's only private house in Kansas is a superb example of his work. It was built for presidential hopeful Henry Allen, governor of Kansas 1919-23. The exterior appearance of a brick Prairie House hides the enclosed garden, terrace, pool and summer house. The interiors are exceptionally rich, with plenty of art-glass and gold leaf.

and she soon began treating him with contempt. In his autobiography - both the first version and the revised edition - Frank praised his mother but depicted his father in a rather unflattering light; it is apparent that he always took his mother's side in any family arguments.

Meanwhile the family had moved to Weymouth, a suburb of Boston, Massachusetts, where William was minister at a Baptist church. At the time, Boston was the undisputed cultural center of America and Anna was able to attend concerts and lectures and buy the latest books. In 1876 they went on vacation to Philadelphia and Anna visited the Centennial Exposition there. At the fair she was introduced to a series of educational toys, called "Gifts," which had been designed for mothers and teachers so they could train children using Froebel's system. Friedrich Froebel was the German inventor of the kindergarten and he had developed a series of exercises to educate a child's sensory experience of the world through play. The "Gifts" consisted of colored strips of paper, two-dimensional geometric grids, and wooden spheres, blocks and pyramids. Children were encouraged to arrange the wooden shapes on the grids to create geometric patterns and structures.

Although both Frank and his sister Jane were much older than the children Froebel's system was aimed at, they were both fascinated by it. Many years later, Frank

Lloyd Wright regularly cited the "Gifts" as one of the biggest influences on his approach to architecture and noted that his habit of designing on a modular plan directly paralleled Froebel's exercises. Throughout his career, Wright habitually used a small number of geometric shapes in different combinations. Froebel also encouraged the children to associate shapes with symbolic meanings, and Wright went along with this. To him, the circle symbolized infinity; the triangle, structural unity; the spire, aspiration; the spiral, organic progress; and the square, integrity. Froebel also believed that his students should not make drawings directly from objects until they had spent many months working on his geometric exercises, which he thought would help them to understand the underlying geometry that structured the appearance of everything in the world. Wright constantly referred to his work as "organic" or "natural," but avoided using any naturalistic designs. Instead he used highly abstract and geometrical patterns, which are the essence of the natural forms they represent but do not look like them. The best-known examples of this are the sumac at the Susan Lawrence Dana House in Springfield (1902) and the hollyhock at the Aline Barnsdall "Hollyhock House" in Los Angeles (1917-21).

In 1878, the Wright family moved to Madison, into a

house on the shores of Lake Mendota. The children were now able to spend the summer months on the Lloyd Jones's family farm at Hillside. The marriage of William and Anna, however, soon completely broke down and William sued for divorce. Anna did not contest and received the house and custody of the children. Soon afterwards the children lost contact with their father and Frank did not seek him out later or attend his funeral.

Although Frank was intelligent and a keen reader, he seemed to find school very difficult. He always had low grades, dropped out several times and failed to graduate from high school. Despite this, he entered the University of Wisconsin as a special student where he was briefly a student-assistant to Ellen D. Conover, the Professor of Engineering. He soon left, but Conover then offered him a job in his architectural practice in Madison, where he was introduced to the rudiments of civil engineering and draftsmanship. As a result, Wright decided to drop out of education entirely and go to Chicago to learn in the "real world."

FOLLOWING PAGE: *Frank Lloyd Wright Home & Studio (Oak Park, Illinois, 1889). Aerial view of Wright's home and studio, showing the overall plan of the building. He was continually adding to and redesigning it as he tried out new ideas, using it as a "living laboratory" of architecture.*

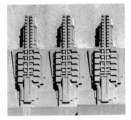

LEFT: Detail of the stylized hollyhock design used throughout Hollyhock House. Wright constantly referred to his work as "organic" or "natural," but used highly abstract and geometrical patterns, which are the essence of the natural forms they represent but do not look like them.

After pawning books left behind by his father, Wright had enough money for a railroad ticket with $7 left for food and lodging until he found a job. According to his autobiography, he spent four days visiting different architectural practices in the city before he was offered a job as a draftsman with Joseph J. Silsbee. By coincidence, Silsbee was the architect on a new church being built by Wright's uncle, Jenkin Lloyd Jones, who was one of the leading preachers in Chicago. Despite this, Wright averred that he did not use his family connection to influence Silsbee and that he was offered the job on the strength of the drawings he had taken to the meeting and on the recommendation of Cecil Corwin, one of Silsbee's draftsmen.

After he got the job, Anna came to Chicago with her two daughters and they settled in Oak Park, so Wright was able to live at home. At first Wright enjoyed working with Silsbee, who had enormous influence on his future life and work. Silsbee often designed in a Queen Ann style - which Wright also used in his early career - and he was fond of Oriental art, particularly Japanese prints, a taste he also passed on to Wright. Despite this, Wright quickly became bored with the "safe" style of the firm's designs and left, but he soon returned as he found himself out of his depth. He did not stay for long, however, as he shortly found himself another position in the drafting rooms of Adler and Sullivan, a much more progressive practice. Louis Sullivan himself hired Wright, as he was looking for a draftsman who could draw in the same style as his own. Perhaps Wright knew this, as the work he presented included several drawings that he had redrawn in Sullivan's style.

Adler and Sullivan were working on the Auditorium Building, which would make them famous across America. By the time it came to be built in 1890, Wright had worked his way up to head draftsman and had his own office next to Sullivan, who he called his *"Lieber Meister."* Around this time, Wright also met Catherine Tobin, the daughter of a wealthy Chicago businessman, at a social gathering at his uncle's church. Despite his mother's objections, she and Wright were soon married - after Wright had secured a five-year contract of employment from Sullivan and a $5000 loan to buy a plot of land and build a house.

The original design of Wright's first house shows the influence of Sullivan, but Wright continuously altered and extended it, using it as a kind of laboratory to try

FOLLOWING PAGE: *Frank Lloyd Wright Home & Studio (Oak Park, Illinois, 1889). In the center is the original house of 1889, with its steep pitched room. To the right is the studio and to the left the drafting room, both added in 1897. There was also a barrel-vaulted playroom added in 1893.*

out new ideas and materials. He also now developed a thriving architectural practice on the side, by picking up all the domestic commissions Adler and Sullivan were too busy to undertake, and doing them himself without his employers' knowledge. These houses, which he called his "bootlegged houses" were done in his own time and did not strictly violate his contract with Adler and Sullivan, but when Sullivan found out they apparently had a furious row. Whatever the truth of the matter, Wright left Adler and Sullivan on less than amicable terms and did not become reconciled with Sullivan for twenty years.

Wright first set up with Cecil Corwin, but after Corwen moved back east, Wright was unable to pay the rent on the offices they had taken. Throughout his life Wright was constantly in debt, no matter how much money he earned, and had a reputation for paying bills late. In 1905, Wright and his wife were invited to accompany the Ward Willits to Japan, and Wright had to borrow $5000 to make the trip - which he later argued about paying back. However, he now had a growing reputation as an architect and had built himself a studio at his Oak Park home, where he worked with a number of assistants. He developed his Prairie House, and built over 30 of them between 1900 and 1910.

In 1909, his life changed entirely. He had made the

Freedom is from within.

An expert is a man who has stopped thinking - he knows!

The truth is more important than the facts.

There is nothing more uncommon than common sense.

The longer I live, the more beautiful life becomes.

Television is bubblegum for the mind.

I believe in God, only I spell it Nature.

Study nature, love nature, stay close to nature.
It will never fail you.

Mechanization best serves mediocrity.

25

mistake of falling in love with the wife of one of his clients, Martha Borthwick Cheney - known as Mamah. They were unable to live together in conservative America, so Wright abandoned his wife and six children and moved to Europe, closely followed by Mamah, who left behind her husband and two children. The ensuing scandal meant that Wright would not be able to work

PREVIOUS PAGE: *Frank Lloyd Wright Home & Studio (Oak Park, Illinois, 1889). Wright's drafting room, a two-storey structure of an octagon above a cube - its form recalling the Froebel "Gifts" Wright experienced as a child. The exterior of the house reflects Wright's interest in the "Shingle" style popular on the East Coast at the time.*

RIGHT: *Frank Lloyd Wright's bedroom at Oak Park, with its arched and beamed ceiling.*

OPPOSITE: *The two-story octagonal drafting room in Wright's house in Oak Park, which was top-lit and had an internal balcony overlooking the central area.*

LEFT: *Walter M. Gale House (Oak Park, Illinois, 1893). A two-story house with a clapboard exterior, one of three houses with identical T-plans on Chicago Avenue in Oak Park. The huge polygonal windows open up the rooms to the outside.*

again in Chicago, as no one wanted to employ a philanderer. The two lovers stayed abroad for a year, living in Berlin while Wright worked on a complete monograph of his work that was being put together by the German publisher Ernst Wasmuth, and going to Florence to spend the winter. They liked Italy so much, that they stayed there for the remainder of their stay. By 1911, the monograph was finished and in a typical flamboyant gesture, Wright purchased the entire print run - it took him many years to recoup this money.

On their return to America, Wright went to Spring Green, Wisconsin, where his mother, Anna, had given them a plot of the family land. It was rocky and unsuitable for farming, but ideal as a site for a rural retreat, and Wright christened it Taliesin, which is Welsh for "shining brow." Despite mounting debts, Wright began building a lavish home there, and after her divorce he was joined by Mamah. Soon commissions did begin coming in, including two of the most important of his career, the Imperial Hotel in Japan and the Midway Gardens complex in Chicago.

Although everything now seemed to be going well, in the summer of 1914 tragedy struck. The cook at Taliesin, Julian Carleton, went mad and set fire to the building, attacking the occupants with an axe as they tried to escape. Mamah, her two children, draftsman Emil Brodelle, Ernest Weston, son of Wright's carpenter

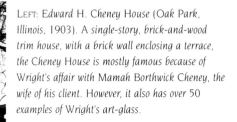

LEFT: Edward H. Cheney House (Oak Park, Illinois, 1903). A single-story, brick-and-wood trim house, with a brick wall enclosing a terrace, the Cheney House is mostly famous because of Wright's affair with Mamah Borthwick Cheney, the wife of his client. However, it also has over 50 examples of Wright's art-glass.

BELOW: The living room is at the center of the plan and opens into the dining room. All the public rooms are at the front of the house, set above street level over a raised basement that housed Mrs. Cheney's sister.

William Weston, and two handymen, David Lindblom and Thomas Brunker all died. Carleton had taken poison and died some weeks later in prison, never revealing what had driven him to such an act. Wright was heartbroken, but vowed to rebuild Taliesin.

As the new Taliesin rose from the ashes of the old, Wright also took a new mistress, a sculptress called Miriam Noel. Their relationship was stormy, because Miriam was artistic but unbalanced, and tremendously insecure. It also had other repercussions - a housekeeper, Nellie Breen, who Wright had dismissed, passed some of Miriam's letters to Wright to the newspapers. Breen then initiated an action in the courts to have Wright charged under the Mann Act - a statute only passed in Congress in 1910, which prohibited the transportation of women across state borders for "immoral purposes." Wright was defended by Clarence Darrow, who succeeded in getting the case dismissed.

When Wright finally achieved his divorce from Catherine in 1922, he and Miriam were married, but six months later they separated, and Wright returned to Taliesin alone. However, in November 1924 he attended the ballet and met Olga Lazovich Hinzenberg, known as Olgivanna, a dancer from a Montenegrin family who had been educated in Tsarist Russia. She was married to the Russian architect Vladimir Hinzenberg, but was

Less is only more when more is no good.

An architect's most useful tools are an eraser at
the drafting board, and a wrecking bar at the site.

Consider everything in the nature of a hanging fixture
a weakness, and naked radiators an abomination.

The space within becomes the reality of the building.

I have been black and blue in some spot, somewhere, almost all
my life from too intimate contacts with my own furniture.

When a client complained that the rain leaked through
the roof of his house onto the dining room table,
Wright replied "Move the chair."

A doctor can bury his mistakes, but an architect
can only advise his clients to plant vines.

RIGHT: Taliesin (Spring Green, Wisconsin, 1925). On his return to America in 1910, Wright was given a plot of family land. It was rocky and unsuitable for farming, but ideal as a site for a rural retreat, and Wright christened it Taliesin, which is Welsh for "shining brow." The current Taliesin was built in 1925, after fire destroyed much of Taliesin I in 1914, and Taliesin II in 1925.

BELOW: Taliesin now denotes the whole complex at Spring Green, although initially it related only to the main house.

divorcing him and fighting for custody of their daughter, Svetlana. Within a few months Olgivanna had moved into Taliesin and the following year produced a daughter for Wright, Iovanna. Olgivanna took over the reins at Taliesin, attending to all the domestic matters so the mind of the great architect was free to reside on a higher plane. Miriam at first refused a divorce and dragged Wright's name through the courts - and Wright was once again charged under the Mann Act after taking Olgivanna for a short holiday after Iovanna's birth.

The flagrant immorality of all these goings-on put off many prospective clients, and work was very short on the ground. In 1925 another fire at Taliesin did thousands of dollars worth of damage to the building, and to Wright's books and drawings. At the insistence of his creditors, Wright's large and valuable collection of

LEFT: Taliesin (*Spring Green, Wisconsin, 1925*). *After the fire of 1925, the original structure evolved into a complex of buildings, which was constantly expanding. From 1937 Taliesin was Wright's summer home, and winters were spent at Taliesin West in Arizona.*

FOLLOWING PAGE: *This part of the complex is one of the oldest, having twice survived destruction by fire. The buildings are now managed by the Frank Lloyd Wright Foundation, and the Visitors' Center is housed in the former Riverview Terrace Restaurant.*

RIGHT AND BELOW: *Ravine Bluffs Housing Development (Glencoe, Illinois, 1915). In 1915, Wright designed a housing development of six houses in Glencoe, called Ravine Buffs, which had been commissioned by Sherman M Booth. The houses were all for rent, and were named after their first tenants: Perry, Root, Kier, Ross and Kissam. As well as the houses themselves, there are also poured concrete sculptures, and a bridge that marks the northeast entrance to the development.*

Japanese prints - which were valued at over $100,000 - were sold at auction for $40,000, which still left him $43,000 in debt. Wright was given a year by the Wisconsin Savings Bank to pay off the outstanding amount, and get Taliesin back. He failed to meet the deadline, but was bailed out by a group of friends and clients, who formed Frank Lloyd Wright Inc., to bankroll Wright and keep him from debt. In 1928 he also finally gained his divorce from Miriam and married Olgivanna, who stayed with him

for the rest of his life and provided a stability that enabled him to focus on his work.

During the great depression of the 1930s there was very little work around but Wright turned his energies to establishing the Taliesin Fellowship, which was

PREVIOUS PAGE: *Charles R. Perry House (Glencoe, Illinois, 1915). A square-plan, three-bedroom plaster and wood house, this is one of the houses located in the Ravine Bluffs development. Its design is derived from the "Fireproof House" idea, to which Wright returned many times.*

ABOVE RIGHT: *Gregor S. Affleck House (Michigan, 1940). The Affleck House is another example of Wright's ability to maximize the dramatic settings of his houses. The living room is built on piers, cantilevered over a basement and garden level, which has seats and a pool.*

RIGHT: *Maynard P. Buehler House (Orinda, California, 1948). An L-plan, exposed concrete-block and wood house, with the sleeping quarters in the long leg and the workspace in the short. Wright's buildings in California span almost 90 years; he maintained an office in Los Angeles, so there are more examples here than anywhere else in the US, except for those states on the shores of the Great Lakes.*

FOLLOWING PAGE: *Arthur C. Mathews House (Atherton, California, 1950). A brick-built house with two parallel wings that emanate from a central dining area segment, producing an enclosed terrace and garden.*

Toleration and liberty are the foundations of a great republic.

I believe totally in a Capitalist system,
I only wish someone would try it.

A free America, democratic in the sense that
our forefathers intended it to be, means just this:
individual freedom for all, rich or poor, or else this system
of government we call democracy is only an expedient
to enslave man to the machine and make him like it.

Bureaucrats: they are dead at 30 and buried at 60.
They are like custard pies; you can't nail them to the wall.

Maybe we can show government how to operate better
as a result of better architecture.

Harvard takes perfectly good plums as students,
and turns them into prunes.

Democracy is the opposite of totalitarianism,
communism, fascism or mobocracy.

conceived as a community of worker-apprentices, who would pay a fee to come and work and live with the great architect. Part of their daily routine was to do chores around the house, as well as working on assigned design projects. They helped to run the office, helping on projects by doing drawing and model making, and some of the best were later given projects to supervise. Now that Wright's aunts were dead, Hillside School was remodeled into quarters for the Fellowship - the classrooms were converted into galleries, a dormitory was built to house the apprentices and the gymnasium was converted into a theater. He also established Taliesin West in Arizona in 1937, to serve as winter quarters for the Fellowship. The building of Fallingwater in 1935 for Edgar Kaufmann and the S.C. Johnson Wax Administration Building in 1936-39 re-established Wright's reputation. His confident use of new materials and building methods impressed the new generation of architects. He also developed the Usonian House in response to the need for good quality, economic housing for middle class families. Usonia was Wright's

FOLLOWING PAGE: *S.C. Johnson Administration Building and Research Tower (Racine, Wisconsin, 1936 & 1944). The tower is of brick and the floors are cantilevered out from a central core, which contains all the elevators and services.*

term for the United States and its culture. He thought the future of domestic housing was in the mass production of components, but believed that these should be used to create individual houses on site to suit the inhabitants - unlike other architects of the day, who believed houses should be built in factories and shipped complete to site.

The 1940s were some of the most productive years of Wright's career and his architecture became both nationally and internationally recognized. The Usonian House flourished and he also unveiled his plans for the Solomon R. Guggenheim Museum in New York. In the last few years of his life he realized an ambition to build a skyscraper - the Price Company Tower in Bartlesville, Oklahoma. He also created several religious buildings,

RIGHT: *Annunciation Greek Orthodox Church (Wauwatosa, Wisconsin, 1956). The domed roof form of this church is a concrete shell, which was originally surfaced with a celestial-blue ceramic mosaic tile. The tiles were later replaced by a synthetic plastic resin roofing material.*

FOLLOWING PAGE: *Taliesin West (Scottsdale, Arizona, 1937-59). After Wright died in April 1959, aged 91, he was first buried near Mamah Cheney and his mother at Taliesin in Spring Green, Wisconsin, but when Olgivanna died in 1985, his ashes mingled with hers in a new grave at Taliesin West.*

including the Beth Sholom Synagogue in Elkins Park, Pennsylvania. In April 1959, aged 91, he survived an operation for an internal obstruction, but died a few days later on April 9. His body was taken from Phoenix, Arizona to Taliesin, Wisconsin, and he was buried near Mamah Cheney and his mother. However, when Olgivanna died in 1985, Wright was disinterred and his ashes mingled with hers in a new grave at Taliesin West, Arizona.

LEFT: *Florida Southern College (Lakeland, Florida, 1938-54). Esplanades - to shelter the students from tropical downpours and the fierce summer sun - were built in 1946 to link all Wright's buildings on the campus; those buildings not linked were built by other architects.*

59

THE EARLY WORK

■ ■ ■

*"Give me the luxuries of life and
I will willingly do without the necessities."*

■ ■ ■

Frank Lloyd Wright's earliest work was to some extent a derivation of the work of leading American architects of the 1880s, whose work was widely published in contemporary magazines. For instance, in 1887, he designed a Unitarian Chapel for a congregation in Sioux City, Iowa, which strongly resembles the church that Silsbee had earlier designed for Wright's uncle, Jenkin Lloyd Jones. In the 1890s, his work became more classical, but the decoration was strongly influenced by Louis Sullivan, for whom Wright worked for five years.

One of Wright's first independent commissions was a building for Hillside Home School - which was a family

LEFT: *James Charnley House (Chicago, Illinois, 1891). The style and simplicity of this house was ahead of its time. It was originally built symmetrically on an east-west axis, but later additions squared off the dining room bay window. The open second-story loggia was a favorite Sullivan device.*

affair, as the school was run by his maiden aunts. However, it was not until he was working for Adler and Sullivan that Wright's architectural career really began. Among his numerous responsibilities in this job were all the commissions for private houses. Adler and Sullivan did large commercial projects and generally were not interested in domestic work, but for diplomatic reasons sometimes they took such commissions on. These were generally given to a junior assistant, but after 1888 most of these projects were done by Wright. The Charnley House in Astor Street, Chicago, built in 1891, is generally accepted to be the first great building in Wright's career. The Charnleys were close friends of Sullivan - in fact they had bought adjacent plots of land near Biloxi in Mississippi on which each planned to build a country retreat. The Charnley's town house was perhaps sketched out by Sullivan and then turned over to Wright to complete - the open second-story loggia was one of Sullivan's favorite devices. The decorative detailing on the wooden trim throughout the house is also very reminiscent of Sullivan's work. The plan of the house is

RIGHT: *James Charnley House (Chicago, Illinois, 1891). The plan of the house is very simple: a stair hall in the center rises to the top of the building and is flanked on each side by two rooms. Sullivan's influence can also be seen in the decorative interior woodwork.*

very simple: a stair hall in the center rises to the top of the building and is flanked on each side by two rooms. As usual in townhouses on cramped city lots, the kitchen was situated in the basement. Wright called the Charnley house "the first modern building" and said that it was in doing this project that he first recognized the decorative value of plain surfaces.

After Wright married Catherine Tobin, their family quickly began to grow and it was not long before he found himself in financial difficulties. He later blamed this on his burgeoning family, but in fact it was mainly due to Wright's own spendthrift habits. Faced with mounting debts, Wright began to take on domestic commissions on the side, doing them at home. In this period ten houses were designed, although only nine were built. Although this work may not have been in breach of his contract with Adler and Sullivan, Wright obviously knew it would not be approved of, since he called them his "bootlegged houses" and had some of them announced in contractor's journals as the work of his friend, Cecil Corwin. The bootlegged houses were for

LEFT: *James Charnley House (Chicago, Illinois, 1891). Detail of the exterior decorative work above the open loggia and around the roof line. The house was restored in the 1930s and alterations included replacing the front wooden steps with brick and enclosing the porches.*

W.S. MacHarg, Chicago (1890); Dr. A.W. Harlan, Chicago (1892); Warren McArthur, Chicago (1892); George Blossom, Chicago (1892); Robert Emmond, LaGrange, Illinois (1892); two identical houses for Thomas H. Gale, Oak Park, Chicago (1892); Walter Gale, Oak Park (1893); Orrin S. Goan, LaGrange (designed 1893, but not built); Peter Goan, LaGrange (1894).

In his autobiography, Wright apologized for the appearance of the bootlegged houses and claimed they looked the way they did because he was unable to supervise their construction personally. Many of them are obviously influenced by Silsbee - for instance he had introduced the Colonial style to Chicago from the east in 1890, and soon afterwards Wright designed the Blossom House in New England Colonial. Its exterior is clad in yellow clapboard with a white trim, and it has a classical

RIGHT: *George Blossom House (Chicago, Illinois, 1892). The plan of this house is square, but with a single story semicircular porch and two-story semicircular extension, in which is the dining room. The curve of its plan is echoed in the archway that leads into the room.*

FOLLOWING PAGE: *One of Wright's "bootleg houses," the Blossom House is a classic example of New England "Colonial," with its clapboard siding. It is built on a symmetrical plan and contrasts sharply with a Prairie-style garage that was built in 1907 at the rear.*

portico, a doorway with a fanlight, and Palladian windows. However there are a few touches that are pure Wright - a low hip roof, projecting eaves replacing the traditional classical cornice, and a massive Roman brick chimney. The McArthur House is a reworking of the Dutch Colonial style. Wright not only designed the building, but all of its fittings and some of the furniture - the first time he was able to put into practice his belief that the architect

RIGHT: *Warren McArthur House (Chicago, Illinois, 1892). Another of Wright's "bootleg" houses, the McArthur House is a reworking of the Dutch Colonial style. Outside, Roman brick was used up to the window sill. The house and stable were both remodeled in 1900.*

FOLLOWING PAGE: *Robert G. Emmond House (Chicago, Illinois, 1892). Originally a clapboard structure, this house has been resurfaced with brick on its lower story. It was designed on a T-plan, set sideways to the street but has been modified considerably and its terraces are now enclosed.*

should design everything.

The two houses for Thomas Gale and the Goan and Emmond houses are all plain frame structures. These houses all have a similar plan - along one side are the front and back parlors and dining room, on the other are the stairs, kitchen and storage closets. Although this was a practical layout for a small house of the time, Wright must have found it quite dated and restricting. He did add oversized, glazed corner polygons to "bring the outside in," which take up most of the wall space inside and are topped with tall, pointed, polygonal roofs. The Walter Gale house has an enormous two-story, semicircular bay - which again is very reminiscent of Silsbee's design for Jenkin Lloyd Jones's church.

Soon after Wright left Adler and Sullivan and began to rent office space with Cecil Corwin, William H. Winslow came to commission a new house in River Forest, a suburb of Chicago to the west of Oak Park. Winslow was a businessman and the president of a large manufacturer of ornamental ironwork. Although he had enjoyed a long and successful business relationship with Adler and Sullivan, he apparently knew that the firm was not interested in domestic projects and he turned to Wright - although Wright was still only 24 at the time. The Winslow House (1893) was Wright's first important independent commission - and shows hints of the Prairie

Houses that followed in its striking broad-eaved hip roof, without any dormer windows. An optical illusion makes the front door appear much smaller than it actually is. The outer walls of the lower story are of dark orange Roman brick, with buff-colored limestone round doors and windows, the upper story is bronze-glazed tiles and the roof is terracotta tiles. All these fall-like tones combine to give the house a warm coloring. The upper story tiles look neutral from a distance, but close to their ornamentation becomes apparent - a detail borrowed from Sullivan, but handled in a more geometric way. The play of light and shadow over the decorative surface of the tiles makes the top story look lighter and less solid than it actually is. On the north side of the house is an arched *porte-cochère* - an indispensable aid to elegant living, which enabled the inhabitants to park and descend from an automobile under cover. Winslow's hobbies were printing and typography, and a studio and press room were incorporated into the stable block at the rear of the house. In its early years, the stable had a tree growing through its roof, with a rather crude gasket of rubber and cloth that was not successful in keeping the roof from leaking.

Not everyone thought the Winslow House was a masterpiece. After it was completed, William Winslow suffered some mild persecution and for a few months he

LEFT: *Winslow House (Chicago, Illinois, 1893). The first independent commission that Wright completed after leaving Adler & Sullivan, the Winslow House features an early version of his octagonal geometry. It is built in Roman brick, stone and plaster and the broad eaves of the hip roof hint at the Prairie Houses to come.*

FOLLOWING PAGE: *Winslow House (Chicago, Illinois, 1893). An optical illusion makes the front door appear much smaller than it actually is. The outer walls of the lower story are of dark orange Roman brick, with buff-colored limestone round doors and windows, the upper story is bronze-glazed tiles and the roof is terracotta tiles.*

changed his routine to avoid traveling to and from his Chicago office on his normal train and having to put up with the remarks of fellow commuters.

Despite its notoriety, the Winslow House brought Wright to the notice of others looking for new houses and he received commissions for several in both Oak Park and River Forest. However, not everyone wanted something new and different. In late 1894, Nathan Moore came to Wright for the design of an "English House" - and what he meant was a mock-Tudor, half-timbered black-and-white house. Wright later claimed that he took the commission because he needed the money, and because he felt challenged by the opportunity to produce something in a style he disliked intensely. To his

RIGHT: *Nathan G. Moore House (Chicago, Illinois, 1895). Although the Moore House was not to Wright's own taste, it enhanced his growing reputation as an architect of residential housing. It was a convenient project for him as it was situated in Forest Road, directly opposite his own home and studio.*

FOLLOWING PAGE: *Nathan G. Moore House (Chicago, Illinois, 1895). A Roman-brick house, which is essentially Tudor, with a hint of Swiss chalet. Wright claimed he disliked the Tudor style intensely, but took the commission because he needed the money - and felt the opportunity was an interesting challenge. It was rebuilt above the first floor after a fire in 1922.*

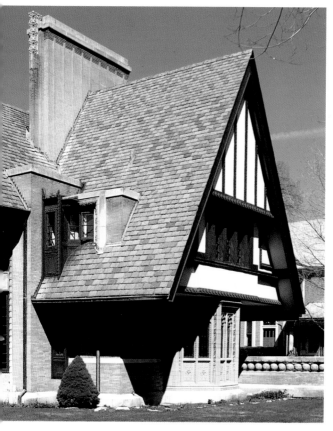

complete horror, the Moore House (1895) was much more popular than the Winslow House, and he had to turn away many clients who all wanted houses in the same style!

Despite his dislike of the Tudor style, he did experiment with it again in the Roloson Houses (1894). These party-wall houses were unique in Wright's work. They were commissioned by Robert Roloson, a son-in-law of Edward Waller, who owned some property on the south side of Chicago. The four identical houses were built to be rented out and provide a return on his investment. The modified Tudor-style buildings designed by Wright have a mezzanine level - the floor level breaks at the central stairwell, so the rooms at the back are several steps lower than those in the front. The interior spaces constantly shift as the floor heights vary, and the main rooms are separated from each other by smaller ante rooms. Outside, the front of the Roloson Houses is dominated by four great gables and the only applied ornament is in the three square spandrels on each

LEFT: *Roloson Rowhouses (Chicago, Illinois, 1894). The first of Wright's "apartment" projects and the only built example of city row houses. Again Wright experimented with the Tudor-style - outside, the front of the building is dominated by four great gables and the only applied ornament is abstract stone work in the three square spandrels on each façade.*

façade. In front of each house is a paved terrace approached by a flight of three steps, and separating the terraces from the sidewalk are balustrades decorated with patterns that are very reminiscent of Sullivan's work.

A much smaller project from around this time had great personal significance for Wright. His aunts needed a windmill to pump water from an artesian well into a newly created reservoir to serve their school. They asked Wright to design something in keeping with their aesthetic ideals, and he sent drawings of a timber and shingled structure. The local builder was convinced it would fall in the first storm, and Wright's aunts sent a concerned telegram asking if he were sure it would stand. Wright's reply just said "Build it." The Romeo and Juliet Windmill (1896) still stands today behind the old Hillside Home School buildings, which are now used as drafting rooms for the Taliesin Fellowship.

Another family commission was less happy - Wright's uncle, Jenkin Lloyd Jones commissioned a new church, as the congregation had outgrown the old one designed by Silsbee. The Abraham Lincoln Center was also to include auditoria, meeting rooms, offices, kitchens, a gym, living quarters for Jenkin Lloyd Jones and his family, and retail shops at ground level to provide income to support the church. Wright produced plans and a model, but he and his uncle clashed repeatedly until Wright turned the project over to his colleague Dwight Perkins, after scribbling on the plans "bldg. completed over protest of architect." The Abraham Lincoln Center finally opened in 1905, but bore little resemblance to Wright's original plans and is never included in lists of his works.

As well as other individual houses, Wright was also involved in two projects for mass housing during the last years of the 19th century. The Francis Apartments (1895), erected in Chicago by the Terre Haute Trust Company of Indiana, were widely admired and often imitated. Wide sash windows and broad bays allowed in sunlight and air, while bands of geometric ornament ran across the cornice and basement course. The ground floor of the north wing contained four shops. The Francisco Terrace (1895), a 44-unit, brick building designed for Edward C. Waller, was a different affair. It was located in a low-income, densely populated area of Chicago known as the "Near West Side" and was intended as good quality but cheap housing. Each pair of apartments had direct access to the outdoors, which did away with inner public corridors. The street front apartments were approached directly from the sidewalk, while those inside faced onto a rectangular central courtyard, which was reached via a single wide archway opening from the street. At each corner of the courtyard were open towers containing public stairways to the second floor. From the stairs,

access to the upper level apartments was via an overhanging walkway that ran along all four sides of the courtyard. Francisco Terrace was occupied solely by young, childless couples and was nicknamed "Honeymoon Court." Since there were no children playing in the central courtyard, the building was relatively quiet and peaceful. After years of neglect and vandalism, Francisco Terrace was demolished in 1974, despite the attempts of local people to save it. However, the archway of cut stone and terracotta and the stairwell

PREVIOUS PAGE: *Fred B. Jones House (Lake Delavan, Wisconsin, 1901). Part of the Delavan Lake Group, the Jones House is the most extensive and has an exterior of board-and-batten siding. The front verandah and the porte-cochère have distinctive arches.*

RIGHT: *Henry Wallis Summer Residence (Lake Delavan, Wisconsin, 1900). Detail of the horizontal board-and-batten siding on the exterior of the Wallis House. The Lake Delavan Group consists of several waterside cottages designed by Wright, which were mainly holiday houses for his clients rather than their main residence.*

FOLLOWING PAGE: *The Wallis Summer Residence is actually a very modest cottage, very similar in style to the later Ward Willits House. The exterior board-and-batten siding has been resurfaced, so the building now looks somewhat different to Wright's original concept.*

motifs were saved and reconstructed in Oak Park, at the entrance to a building on Euclid Place and Lake Street, which had similar exterior design to the original Francisco Terrace Building, although it is smaller in scale. Wright also designed a second set of apartments for Waller in Chicago, which were of better quality.

Apart from domestic projects, Wright also undertook the designs for several public structures in these early years, which were mostly never built. These include the Wolf Lake and Cheltenham Beach resorts, the remodeling of the Mozart Gardens, a road-house popular with cyclists, the competition design for a bank sponsored by *Brickbuilder*, and a proposed office building for the American Luxfer Prism Company. The American Luxfer Prism Company made prismatic glass bricks, and wanted to popularize them as replacements for traditional glazed windows in commercial structures like offices and factories. Wright designed a 10-story headquarters building for them, the façade of which was filled with 48 squares of prismatic glass - the forerunner of modern glass-box office buildings. Shortly after designing their building, Wright negotiated a contract with the company to act as their architectural consultant.

The long-demolished River Forest Golf Club (1898) was the only clubhouse Wright designed during this period, but it was a forerunner of several to come. The central feature of the building was the large octagonal common room, which was added when the club was enlarged in 1901. From this central room, wings extended forwards and sideways, turning back on themselves and enclosing two small courtyards. With its very low, widely overhanging hip roofs, ribbon windows and bands of masonry and shingle, the River Clubhouse was the closest Wright got to the Prairie House in this early period.

In the early 1900s, Wright built several waterside cottages on Lake Delavan in Wisconsin, as holiday houses for clients. The Fred B. Jones House (1901) is the most extensive of the Lake Delavan projects: the site includes a gate lodge, a barn with stables and a boathouse. The exterior of the main house is of board and batten siding, while the interior features a large Roman brick fireplace. The living room has a staircase leading to a balcony, which overlooks it and other rooms. It has distinctive arches on the front verandah and at the *porte-cochère*. The Henry Wallis Summer House (1900) is much more modest, and is similar in style to the Ward Willits House (1901) in Highland Park, Illinois. The Ward Willets House is generally accepted to be the first Prairie House Wright designed - although it was not the first to be built - as it was during the first years of the 20th century that he developed the concept.

THE PRAIRIE HOUSE

■ ■ ■

*"True ornament is not a matter of prettifying externals. It is
organic with the structure it adorns, whether a person, a building,
or a park. At its best it is an emphasis of structure, a realization
in graceful terms of the nature of that which is ornamented."*

■ ■ ■

While still living in Oak Park, Wright began to test his
ideas on the use of space to achieve a flowing, unified
effect and came up with the concept of the Prairie
House. The Ward Willits House (1901) is claimed as the
first true Prairie House to be designed, but several years
passed before it was built so the first to be erected were
probably those for Warren Hickox (1900) and Harley
Bradley (1900). There is no doubt about the public
unveiling of the concept, however.

In 1900, the president of Curtis Publishing, Edward
Bok, had launched a project to improve the design of
American houses - particularly with regard to sanitation

LEFT: *W.R. Heath House (Buffalo, New York, 1905). A T-plan Prairie
House, faced with dark red Roman brick and russet tiles. Although 1905
was the year Wright went to Japan, there is little evidence of it in this
Prairie-style house.*

and efficiency. Bok was a champion of hygiene in the home and believed strongly in airy sleeping porches, sanitary bathrooms and kitchens, and servants quarters of a humane size. Bok invited numerous architects to contribute designs, to be published in the *Ladies' Home Journal*, of houses that could be constructed at a price that was within reach of its readers. A complete set of working drawings for the houses would be offered for public sale at only $5 per set. Many architects refused Bok's invitation, claiming it was beneath their dignity to engage on such a venture. Wright, however, jumped at the opportunity to demonstrate that the best quality housing could be available to the greatest number of people at the lowest cost possible. It was in these designs that Wright officially unveiled the Prairie House: the title of the first drawing, published in February 1901,

RIGHT: W.R. Heath House (Buffalo, New York, 1905). Detail of the exterior, showing the dark red Roman bricks. Heath was the company attorney of the Larkin Company and was a good friend of Wright's when he lived in Oak Park.

FOLLOWING PAGE: The large eastern porch is an entrance to the living room, which also has windows to the south. The north wall of the living room is dominated by the fireplace - Wright believed that the hearth was the "sacred heart" of a building, signifying family life.

was "A Home in a Prairie Town." These are fully-fledged Prairie Houses, except that they do not include the leaded casement windows in order to keep the price down. Wright's two houses were scaled down to meet the included itemized budgets. The first house was costed at $7,000; the second design, published in July 1901, was called "A Small House with Lots of Room in It" and was estimated at around $5,800.

In the plan of the first house, the interior partitions are reduced to the bare minimum and, where possible, replaced by head-height screens that indicate, without actually fixing, the function of the space and how people might move through it. The ground floor plan is thus a single space in which the dining and living areas and a library are accommodated. An alternative sketch substitutes two bedrooms for the original balcony over the unified living area. In the second design, in place of the now customary low hip roofs, there are gables - a feature that would mark Wright's work until 1906. He appears to have recognized that the average homemaker was attached to this traditional pointed roof shape.

Despite the fact that the designs were published in a nationally-read magazine, the general effect on American homemakers was not immediate. Apart from one commission for the Sutton House at McCook in Nebraska, no others came into the studio as a direct result of the publication of the drawings, and the *Ladies' Home Journal* designs essentially remained paper plans. However, the Hickox and Bradley Houses, with their low, broad gables, are similar in appearance to the second published design - although both were more "tailor-made" in details and fixtures.

Soon afterwards, Wright designed two houses for his Oak Park friends, Frank Thomas and Arthur Heurtley. Both the Thomas and the Heurtley Houses have their main rooms on the second floor, while the ground floor takes the place of the old-fashioned basement - Wright disliked both the basements and attics of traditional architecture. The Heurtley House uses a pinwheel plan in which the various elements "revolve" around a central hall, within a rectilinear configuration. The principle was based on a natural growth pattern, the spiral, which in rectilinear form becomes a pinwheel. The house has a broad, sheltering roof - almost identical to the roofs of the Thomas and Winslow Houses - and orange-colored brick walls, which are laid in bands of regularly projecting and receding courses that create a strong horizontal effect. The horizontal theme is further accentuated by the screen-like windows, whose rhythm is punctuated by wooden mullions. The front entrance is reached through a Romanesque arch. Inside space is allowed to flow continuously in the L-shape formed by

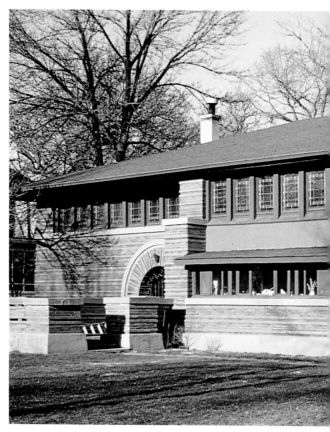

PREVIOUS PAGE: Arthur Heurtley House (Oak Park, Illinois, 1902).
Heurtley commissioned this house at the same time as his summer cottage
in Michigan was being remodeled. The front entrance is reached through a
Romanesque arch, similar to that used in the Dana House.

ABOVE: Ward W. Willits House (Highland Park, Illinois, 1901).
A classic example of Wright's Prairie House style, the Willits House has a
living room dominated by the floor-to-ceiling glazing of the end wall. It is
constructed from wood and steel, with exterior plasterwork and wood trim,
and the living quarters are slightly raised above ground level. Each wing
comes off the central core in a pinwheel configuration.

the living and dining areas, both of which are linked to the hall at first floor level.

At the same time that the Heurtley House was being built, Wright was supervising the construction of what many consider to be the first masterpiece of the Prairie Houses: the Ward W. Willets House (1901). The Willits House presents a formal, almost symmetrical façade to the street and established a precedent for Prairie Houses with symmetrical wings. The long, low-roofed *porte-cochère* at the front entrance balances the low-roofed porch at the end of the dining room. Inside, the ground floor rooms - living, dining, pantry and kitchen - pinwheel off the massive central chimney. Behind the kitchen are a flight of service stairs, two servant's bedrooms and a bathroom. On the second floor, off a narrow corridor, are three fitted bedrooms, two further bathrooms, a large nursery and a linen room. The main staircase rises through the double height space: on the landing is a library, while on the floor below is a small reception room.

Once building commenced, Wright continued to refine and improve the designs for the house - seeing the spaces develop in three dimensions often gave him additional ideas. The Willits House is evidence of this in practice; in construction photographs, the second floor west wall of the south wing is all on one plane, but the

PREVIOUS PAGE: *Susan Lawrence Dana House (Springfield, Illinois, 1902). Sometimes known as the Dana-Thomas House in recognition of extensive restoration work by Mr. and Mrs. Charles C. Thomas in 1944. It is designed on a cruciform plan and incorporates part of the earlier house on its site into the structure. A Prairie-style building, it is the first example to feature Wright's characteristic two-story high living room.*

RIGHT: *Detail of the front entrance. The house is connected to the Lawrence Memorial Library on the same site by a covered passage that also doubled as a conservatory.*

house as it exists today shows that this wall was relocated about three feet further west. If left as originally planned, the stair hall would have been unextraordinary, but the enlargement makes it an impressive space. Entering via the low entrance, the space dramatically opens up to a two-story chamber topped by an art-glass ceiling light and a statue of the Victory of Samothrace. It was a scheme he was to use again, in the Susan Lawrence Dana House. As in all the finest of Wright's houses, the Willits House contains many fine details: the jewel-like glass; the furniture; the wooden screens that divide the space between rooms and encourage passage from one space to another - and of course the massive fireplace, the physical and spiritual center of the home.

110

The Dana House (1902-4) was Wright's most extravagant commission to date. Mrs. Susan Lawrence Dana had originally wanted the old family Victorian mansion

LEFT: *Susan Lawrence Dana House (Springfield, Illinois, 1902). Detail of the wall fountain in the entrance hallway, "The Moon Children," by Richard Bock, which has art-glass screens behind it featuring the sumac motif. There is a great deal of art glass in the building, as well as other sculptures by Bock.*

INSET: *The sumac motif is used to unify the overall design and appears throughout the Dana House - a variant on it is used in the design of the metal and colored glass pendant lamps.*

113

to be remodeled and enlarged in an Italianate style, but as the design and building work progressed, remnants of the old house gradually diminished. The Lawrences had been a pioneer family in central Illinois and by the 20th century had become sufficiently established in society in Springfield. Mrs. Dana now wanted a house that was both a family home and a tribute to the family - past present and future. She was both wealthy and eccentric - as well as being a suffragette and a philanthropist, she kept in touch by spirit guide with her deceased father, whose guidance was sought on all practical and financial matters.

The plan of the Dana House is based on a series of grand rooms: a two-story high dining room, a library, and an art gallery housed in a detached building linked by a pergola to the long arm of the T-shaped plan of the main house. The rooms were designed to accommodate social gatherings of several hundred of Mrs. Dana's closest friends - and for those who tired of the highbrow talk at her parties, there was always the bowling alley in the basement.

The original Lawrence house had stood on a plot that was several feet higher than the level of Fourth Street, which it faced. The new house, with its broad, low-modeled gables flashed with copper, maintained the elevated position but had a new entrance cut from

Lawrence Street - named naturally enough after one of Springfield's most prominent families. The visitor approaches the entrance via a flight of low steps, through two Romanesque archways and under a vaulted space filled with art glass depicting stylized wild flowers common to the Midwest - sumac, purple aster and goldenrod - which harmonized with the overall palette of the house. Outside, buff-colored Roman bricks are set off by a band of bronze luster tiles. Inside, oak furniture is combined with brown and russet fabrics. In addition to the decorative accessories, the furniture, fixtures, fittings and textiles were all made to Wright's design specifications.

Part of the house is designed on the raised basement principle, and halfway between basement and first floor is the entrance landing. On this stands a terracotta obelisk, designed by Wright and executed by Richard Bock, called "Flower in the Crannied Wall" after a line by Tennyson. As the obelisk tapers to its apex, it is transformed into the figure of an idealized female nude, who is placing the finishing touches to the finials of a skyscraper. At the landing, visitors are offered the option of descending via the main staircase to a bathroom and a long passage leading to the library, or ascending to the salon, dining room, living room, Mrs. Dana's mother's bedroom, the art gallery and a study. The study was that

PREVIOUS PAGE: William E. Martin (Oak Park, Illinois, 1902). A three-story house of plaster with a wood trim, this is a precursor of the Prairie Houses to come. It was restored to a single family house in 1945, after many years of being split into three apartments.

RIGHT: Darwin D. Martin House (Buffalo, New York, 1904). The glass work in this house was by Orlando Gianinni, who collaborated with Wright on many projects during this period.

of the late Mr. Lawrence (Mrs. Dana's father) and had been retained from the old house and incorporated into the new. A second, impressive flight of stairs leads to Mrs. Dana's bedroom, two guest rooms, two servant's rooms, several bathrooms and to a narrow balcony that overlooks the vaulted, two-story dining room. Outside, behind a two-story wood and masonry screen was the garden and a reflecting pool.

The contrast between the much smaller, jewel-like Heurtley House and the palatial Dana House demonstrates the adaptability of the Prairie House formula. They could be simple or complex, one or two storys, made of masonry or a light frame structure, be faced in stucco, brick, stone or shingle. The Prairie House was also equally at home in the neat city suburbs with their carefully manicured lawns, in the middle of a forest or the edge of the Great Lakes.

The William E. Martin House (1902) was a narrow, three-story Prairie House in Oak Park for the president of the Martin and Martin Stove Polish Company of Chicago, manufacturers of the E-Z brand of stove polish. The house is generally regarded as being the least successful of Wright's houses, as the site is too small to do justice to the Prairie House formula, but the commission was important as it marked the beginning of Wright's involvement with the Martin family. William Martin's brother, Darwin, lived in Buffalo, New York, and he was so impressed with the house that Wright had designed for his brother that he commissioned him to design and build two houses on his land in a new development in Buffalo. Darwin D. Martin was also chief attorney of the Larkin Company, a job he had taken over from William R. Heath, also bringing in Walter V. Davidson as Advertising Manager. Wright's connection with the Martin brothers eventually led to nine commissions: the William E. Martin House; the Darwin D. Martin House (1904); the W.R. Heath House (1905); the Barton House (1903); the Walter Davidson House

LEFT: *Darwin D. Martin House (Buffalo, New York, 1904). This building, with its original conservatory, is a large, T-plan house. It is one of the largest Prairie Houses and was constructed from russet Roman brick, with oak trim.*

121

(1908); the Darwin D. Martin Summer House (1927); the Larkin Building (1903); the E-Z Polish Factory (1905) and an exposition building for the Jamestown Tercentennial of 1907.

The two houses Darwin D. Martin wanted in New York were both on a large area of land he owned in Jewitt Parkway, one for himself and one for his sister and brother-in-law, the George Bartons. Although Martin commissioned it, this second house is always known as the Barton House. The main part of the Darwin D. Martin House is a low, two-story block: on the left is the *porte-cochère*, on the right a covered porch. Bisecting the house is the entrance hall and to its right is a large room, divided by partitions. The central space functions as the living room and has a huge, wide fireplace. The two flanking spaces serve as the dining room and a library. These two rooms are light-filled spaces because of the long rows of windows, but the living room is darker as it is in the shadow of the roof of the porch. As an afterthought, Wright cut a skylight through the floor of the bedroom gallery directly above the living room to increase the amount of light. To the left of the hall are a second living room, Martin's private office, toilets and the kitchen.

The house is heated by banks of shoulder-height radiators housed in perforated oak cupboards and the space between the top of the cupboards and the ceilings is filled with small leaded casement windows, which open into adjoining rooms. As in the Dana House, Wright was given an unrestricted budget in the Darwin D. Martin House, and he created one of the most complete Prairie House interiors: light fixtures, rugs, hangings, furniture - even the grand piano - were all designed by Wright.

The smaller Barton House - built of the same warm red Roman brick - was the first of the pair to be built and it reduces the Prairie House formula to a strict symmetrical plan. This house has its side entrance on Summit Street, and - along with the communal greenhouse and garage - is set behind the Martin House, but is joined to it by a long pergola. As well as unifying the plan, the pergola also provides protected access to the greenhouse and divides the garden from the kitchen yards. Contained in the pergola's basement are steam pipes used for heating the two homes, with the furnace housed in the garage.

The years between 1905 and 1910 were the heyday of the Prairie House. During that time nearly two thirds of them - some 40 house - were designed. Some were planned for limited budgets, using mass-production techniques and with the usual Wrightian decoration scaled down to reduce costs. Examples of this type of

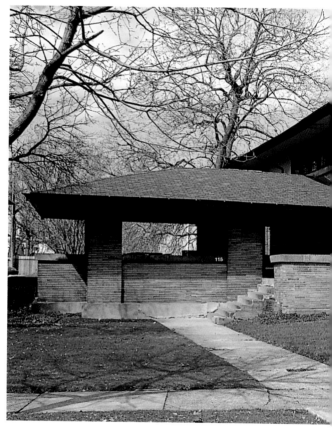

PREVIOUS PAGE: *George Barton House (Buffalo, New York, 1903). Built on a cruciform plan, the dining room of this house is situated to the west, the living room east, the kitchen north and the entrance - with verandah - to the south. George Barton was the brother-in-law of Darwin D. Martin, and their houses were on adjoining sites. It was very carefully restored during the 1970s.*

RIGHT: *P.D. Hoyt House (Geneva, Illinois, 1906). A Prairie-style house, this is built on a square plan and demonstrates the versatility of Wright's concept, which was scaled down to match the limited budget. The exterior walls have a plastered surface with a dark-stained wood trim.*

FOLLOWING PAGE: *Stephen M.M. Hunt House I (LaGrange, Illinois, 1907). This is the best example of "A Fireproof House," as advertised in 1907, to be built. It was originally designed to be constructed in concrete, which would have made it fireproof, but was actually built in wood and plaster. The original terraces have been enclosed, but the oak woodwork and the Tiffany brick fireplace have been fully restored.*

Prairie House include the Sutton House (McCook, Nebraska, 1905); the Hunt House (LaGrange, Illinois, 1907); the Adams House (Highland Park, Illinois, 1905); the Fuller House (Glencoe, Illinois, 1906), and the Hoyt House (Geneva, Illinois, 1906).

The Hunt and Hoyt Houses are examples of the Prairie House reduced to its most economic form for

popular housing: the simple cube. The square plan, however, remained the exception in Wright's work until much later on. At this time he never used it if the budget permitted an alternative scheme. The windows of these small houses were sometimes leaded in simple geometric patterns; more often than not they were subdivided by wooden mullions into the more conventional squares and diamonds. Where budgets permitted, Wright sometimes included "Tiffany Bricks," a term used at the time to describe light brown Roman bricks with small, dark vitreous marks and holes caused by silicon fusing during firing. Because of their antique, mottled color, the bricks resemble the glass produced by Louis Comfort Tiffany. These bricks were often used for facing the chimneys in the living rooms of Wright's low-budget houses.

The medium-priced Prairie Houses included the

LEFT: *Hiram Baldwin House (Kenilworth, Illinois, 1909). Main entrance.*

FOLLOWING PAGE: *The Prairie-style Baldwin House has an interior that has been extensively remodelled. The idea for the Prairie House was first published as a design for "A Home in a Prairie Town" in the* Ladies' Home Journal *of February 1901. It was in response to a challenge to design houses that could be constructed at a price that was within reach of its readers.*

Isabel Roberts House (River Forest, 1908); the Walter Davidson House (Buffalo, 1908), the Steffens House (Chicago, 1909) and the unbuilt Guthrie House (Sewanee, Tennessee, 1908). This price bracket allowed for a more horizontal treatment and was capable of enlargement, and while some were two stories tall, others were bungalows. The blending of the Prairie House principles with the bungalow was something with which Wright had first experimented in the design of the house for Edwin and Mamah Cheney in Oak Park, Illinois, in 1903.

Finally there were two outstanding Prairie Houses of this period, whose size and quality place them in a class all by themselves: The Avery Coonley House (Riverside, Illinois, 1907) and the Robie House (Chicago, 1906). The Coonley House was the product of a rare mix of a progressive and enlightened client with an unlimited

RIGHT: *Hiram Baldwin House (Kenilworth, Illinois, 1909). Detail of the exterior, a typical Prairie-style house.*

FOLLOWING PAGE: *Charles E. Brown House (Evanston, Illinois, 1905). With a rectangular plan and an open front porch, this house is built with horizontal board-and-batten, with plaster under the eaves and between the top-story windows. The unusual double-hung windows are a rarity in Wright designs.*

LEFT: *Charles E. Brown House (Evanston, Illinois, 1905). This house has many interesting features, including a beautiful Roman brick fireplace in the living room and an early example of mechanical air conditioning.*

budget and a belief in the ability of their chosen architect. According to Wright's autobiography, the Coonleys had examined every project that he had built to that date before contacting him. Seeing this as a compliment, Wright stated that he put his best work into the Coonley House. The building was perfectly suited to its site:

Riverside was laid out in 1869 by Frederick Law Olmsted, at the instigation of the Chicago, Burlington, and Quincy Railroad as a model suburb. The perfectly flat land was cut by an irregular, winding street plan. The Coonley House was planned for a roughly triangular plot at the edge of the Olmsted plan, and was nearly surrounded by the meanders of the Desplaines River. The nature of the terrain is mirrored in the meandering layout of the main house, garages and outbuildings.

In the long, U-shaped plan of the house, two of Wright's strongest beliefs were put into practice: the centrifugal plan and the raised basement. All the main rooms of the house - except for the large, centrally located children's playroom - are on the second level above ground height and every room that is devoted to

RIGHT: *Walter V. Davidson House (Buffalo, New York, 1908). A typical Prairie House of plaster with a dark wood trim, the Davidson House is built on a cruciform plan with its two-story high living room facing south.*

enjoyment looks out over lawns and the garden from a carefully calculated height. The outer walls have a banded effect: the lower parts are coasted in a creamy-colored fine sand plaster, while the upper parts are faced with bronze-colored tiles with a geometric surface pattern. The most frequently published view of the Coonley House is of the front garden with its terraces,

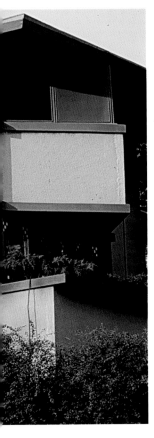

huge, shallow Wrightian planters, and the beautiful reflecting pool.

Inside the Coonley House is zoned within the U-shaped plan: the living and dining rooms, together with the service areas, are located in the western half of the U, while the bedrooms are located in the eastern half. In order that both the family or communal rooms and the master bedrooms should look out onto the gardens to the south, the central bar of the U is divided between living and

LEFT: *Eugene A. Gilmore (Madison, Wisconsin, 1908). Exterior elevation, showing the art-glass used in the windows. Wright had first experimented with the use of art glass in his own house and studio in Oak Park - particularly in the children's playroom built in 1893.*

PREVIOUS PAGE: *Eugene A. Gilmore (Madison, Wisconsin, 1908). This house was originally built on cruciform plan with a massive sitting room, but it was substantially altered in 1928. It is commonly known as "Airplane House."*

RIGHT: *Isabel Roberts House (River Forest, Illinois, 1908). Again designed on a cruciform plan, this building has the usual Prairie House two-story high living room. It was originally constructed of wood surfaced with plaster but was remodeled in 1955, when the exterior was resurfaced with brick veneer and Philippine mahogany was used in the interior. The south porch of the building is built around a tree.*

sleeping quarters. Inside, a harmony of shapes and textures has been created by the furniture and fittings, all of which were designed by Wright. The color scheme is in Wright's preferred hues: natural oak, browns, russets with touches of gold, and greens, all of which is enriched by the light which falls through the leaded casements, and by the ceiling lights. Because of its sheer size and its custom-built furnishings, the Coonley House was a long-term project and even after completion a major alteration was made. It was decided that gaining access directly to the outside from the playroom - the space directly beneath the living room - was too difficult and a row of French doors opening onto the reflecting pool were installed, where originally there

ABOVE: *Avery Coonley House (Riverside, Illinois, 1907). An outstanding example of the Prairie House, this was Wright's first work using the zoned*

148

*plan. It has raised living quarters, which look out over the garden, with a
pavilion linking the various different spaces.*

had been three low windows under a continuous lintel. In 1911, a second major addition was made in the shape of the Avery Coonley Playhouse, a small building built in the grounds and designed to serve as a playhouse and gathering place for neighborhood children.

While the Coonley House setting was largely rural - almost literally in a Midwestern Prairie landscape - the Robie House was Wright's consummate Prairie House adapted to an urban site, although when it was erected Chicago's south side was a somewhat leafier suburb than today. Frederick C. Robie was a

RIGHT: *Avery Coonley House (Riverside, Illinois, 1907). Aerial view - the house was perfectly suited to its site, on a roughly triangular plot. The main house, the garages and outbuildings seem to meander across the landscape.*

successful bicycle manufacturer, engineer and amateur automobile designer. According to Robie, he had sketched out a few ideas and shown them to several builders who told him that what he really wanted was one of "those damn Wright houses." The house that Wright designed for Robie satisfied both client and architect, and fully integrated the elements of design that had been developed in earlier Prairie Houses. In the Robie House, Wright eliminated the basements and set the building on a concrete base. Brick piers and steel beams provided the structural framework upon which the three tiers of the house rest. The landmark, low-hipped roof with its wide projecting eaves - 20-foot wide cantilevered terrace roofs - continues to impress viewers. The overall horizontality of the house is

155

reinforced by the narrow bricks with raked mortar joints. With no room for a garden, Wright ingeniously landscaped nature into the massive planters and urns and at each level doors and windows open onto terraces, balconies and porches, extending the interiors outside and bringing nature inside.

The Robie House is arranged along a single axis, running parallel to the long dimension of the corner lot it inhabits. Integral to the building is the garage - perhaps for the first time in American architecture. Wright, like Robie, had a fascination for automobiles and this may explain why the garage accommodates not one but three cars and has an engine pit and a car wash.

Nicknamed "The Battleship," perhaps because many saw the three levels as "decks" and the projecting terraces as "prows," the entrance to the Robie House is

PREVIOUS PAGE: *George C. Stewart House (Montecito, California, 1909). The designs for the Stewart House were completed shortly before Wright left for Europe and a lovely drawing of it appears in the 1910 Wasmuth Portfolio of Wright's work.*

RIGHT: *George C. Stewart House (Montecito, California, 1909). The first of Wright's Californian houses, the Stewart House is a Midwestern Prairie House set on the Pacific Coast. It is a two-story building, covered with redwood boarding.*

PREVIOUS PAGE: *William B. Greene House (Aurora, Illinois, 1912).
The plaster surface, wood trim and hipped roof of this building are all
common elements of Wright's work in Illinois. The house was extended in
1926 and an enclosed porch was added in 1961.*

LEFT: *By 1912 the design of the Prairie Houses had become increasingly
asymmetrical, reaching out towards some real, or imagined, prairie
horizon. If possible, Wright also liked to design every detail of the interior -
including furniture, fittings, carpets and lights.*

hidden on the north side of the building. Inside areas
that demand privacy - guest bedrooms, kitchen,
servants' rooms - are located in a parallel block at the
rear of the main block. The living room, central staircase
and the dining room create a single unit, separated but
not divided by the chimney. The master bedrooms are
contained in the smaller area of the third level of the
house, a sort of glazed loggia topped by the low,
umbrella-like roof.

Wright, once again, designed the Robie House in its
entirety: the interiors rich with furnishings, light fixtures,
rugs and magnificent art glass. The house, including the
land on which it stands, cost Robie the princely sum of
$59,000. However, just two years later he was forced to
sell when both his marriage and his business failed. In
1957 the Robie House was facing demolition, but was

PREVIOUS PAGE: *Frederick R. Robie House (Chicago, Illinois, 1906). Designated a National Landmark, the Robie House is the best example of the Prairie House in masonry. Everything is integrated to create one of the most imposing buildings of the 20th century.*

LEFT: *Frederick R. Robie House (Chicago, Illinois, 1906). The Robie House is one of the most important examples of the Prairie style, but Frederick Robie - a prosperous young bicycle manufacturer - only lived in it with his family for two and a half years before he had to sell it on. It is enriched inside with furnishings, art-glass, and built-in fixtures.*

saved by a property company who later transferred ownership to the University of Chicago. Now the Robie House is one of the 17 structures designed by Wright to have earned special recognition from the American Institute of Architects as representative of his contribution to American culture.

According to Wright, his "last Prairie House" was designed for Herbert F. Johnson, owner of the S.C. Johnson Wax Company. Wright called the Johnson House "Wingspread" (1937) because the plan consisted of four wings extended in a pinwheel fashion from a high-ceilinged, polygonal central space - which Wright

LEFT: *Frederick R. Robie House (Chicago, Illinois, 1906). The furniture, light fixtures, rugs and magnificent art-glass were all designed by Wright, who described his client as a man with "unspoiled instincts and untainted ideals."*

likened to a wigwam - housing an enormous chimney with five fireplaces on two levels. Each of the wings has a different function: one holds the master bedrooms, another the children's bedrooms and playroom, the third guest rooms and garages and the fourth servants' quarters and services. At the point where the chimney emerged through the sloping, tiled roof, Wright placed a small glass observatory designed to serve as a sort of tree house for the Johnson children. At 14,000 square feet, "Wingspread" is an exceedingly large mansion. The focal point of the living space remains the "sacred hearth," the heart of the home. Inside the warm brick and oak tones are bathed in light from three bands of clerestory windows, set into a circle around the roof. The

library area features Wright's built-in furniture: sofa, coffee tables and octagonal ottomans. A circular staircase leads to the mezzanine, from which the observatory is accessed via a metal spiral staircase.

ABOVE: *Frederick R. Robie House (Chicago, Illinois, 1906). The Prairie Houses became increasingly open with spaces flowing into one another. Here the fireplace provides the only separation between the living and dining rooms. The living room also has beautiful art-glass windows.*

ABOVE: *Herbert F. Johnson House "Wingspread" (Racine, Wisconsin, 1937). The last of the Prairie Houses, Wright always considered this the best. At the point where the chimney emerged through the sloping, tiled roof, he placed a small glass observatory designed to serve as a sort of tree house for the Johnson children.*

LEFT: *The central, octagonal area is three stories high, with a chimney reaching the hull height. The metal spiral staircase behind it provides access to the observatory.*

At the beginning of the 1900s concrete was already being used in construction, although many considered it to be merely a cheap and inferior substitute for masonry. Wright was excited by its possibilities, however, and he soon began to experiment with different ways of using it.

ABOVE: *Herbert F. Johnson House "Wingspread" (Racine, Wisconsin, 1937). Built on a pinwheel plan - a variant of the cruciform - the four wings extend from the central octagon.*

RIGHT: *The focal point of the living space remains the "sacred hearth," the heart of the home. Inside the warm brick and oak tones are encircled by light from three bands of clerestory windows, set into a circle around the roof. Wright also designed built-in furniture and octagonal ottomans.*

WORKING IN
NEW MATERIALS

■ ■ ■

"Every great architect is - necessarily - a great poet.
He must be a great original interpreter of his time,
his day, his age."

■ ■ ■

As early as 1900, Wright had envisaged using concrete, in the plan for "A Village Bank" that was published in B*rickbuilder* magazine in 1901. His first experiment in using reinforced concrete was on the E-Z Polish Building, built for the Martin brothers on Chicago's West Side in 1905. At this time, few buildings in America had been constructed in the material - and those that had were usually heavily disguised with decorative façades and ornamentation that hid the steel and concrete substructure

In the 1920s, Wright began to develop a standardized system of building with pre-cast concrete blocks. Between 1922 and 1932 he worked on at least 30

LEFT: *Aline Barnsdall "Hollyhock House" (Los Angeles, California, 1917).*
Detail of the playhouse windows, showing the distinctive hollyhock color
palette that is used throughout.

projects, five of which were to be realized. According to Wright's autobiography, the idea of building with concrete blocks formed gradually, after he had returned from Japan in 1922; he had been living and working there for five years on the Imperial Hotel project in Tokyo. With the hotel complete, further hopes for major commissions in Japan failed to materialize and Wright returned to the United States. Immediately upon his return, Wright went to Taliesin and remained there for five months.

The exact reason for Wright's decision to relocate to California is not known and in his autobiography he sheds little light on the event. It is likely that a number of factors led to the move: he had been ill with dysentery in Tokyo and was physically exhausted; he was still married to Catherine and his relationship with Miriam Noel was under increasing strain. Consequently, the opportunity to relocate to a sunny climate and a state where large tracts of land for building were available at very low prices may have appeared to Wright to offer a "new beginning" - both in his professional life and personally.

Furthermore, Wright had already built one house on the West Coast. The design for the George C. Stewart House (Montecito, Santa Barbara, 1909) was completed in the Oak Park Studio a few months before Wright's notorious flight to Europe with his mistress, Mamah Borthwick Cheney. Because of his sudden departure, the construction of the Stewart House went unsupervised and numerous changes were made to Wright's original plans - the service wing was enlarged, the attached garage was reworked into a kitchen and the open second floor sleeping balconies were glassed in. Nevertheless, Wright included a perspective drawing of the house in the Wasmuth portfolio published in Berlin in 1910 - the avowed purpose of his trip to Europe.

Since 1920, Wright had also maintained an office in Los Angeles, which was staffed by his son, Lloyd Wright, and Rudolph Schindler, who had begun working for Wright in 1917. To a large extent, Lloyd Wright and Schindler were responsible for overseeing the realization of Wright's second - and probably most recognized - California design. The Aline Barnsdall House, better known as the "Hollyhock House," was begun in 1917 and continued until 1921 - years that, for the most part, Wright spent in Tokyo.

Shortly after Mamah Borthwick Cheney's death in the fire that engulfed Taliesin, Wright met Aline Barnsdall in Chicago. An heiress to millions and a self-proclaimed "new woman," Barnsdall had taken over the running of a small theater in the city. A woman convinced that she could change the world, Barnsdall found Chicago

PREVIOUS PAGE: *Aline Barnsdall "Hollyhock House" (Los Angeles, California, 1917). The "Hollyhock House" is one of Wright's best-known works. Her young daughter, Aline Elizabeth, had her own suite of rooms, as well as this low-ceilinged playhouse in the grounds.*

RIGHT: *Aline Barnsdall "Hollyhock House" (Los Angeles, California, 1917). View of the Hollyhock House living room, showing the hearth and the recreated sofa-table with its integral hollyhock-motif lamp. The house is centered on the living room, and it leads out onto an enclosed garden court that once held a circular reflecting pool.*

somewhat less receptive to her theatrical ideas than she had hoped. Seeking a new audience for her works, she purchased a 36-acre plot of land in East Hollywood, Los Angeles and commissioned Wright to design the house that was to be named after her favorite flower. It was to sit at the top of "Olive Hill" - Barnsdall also named the hill - and look out over olive and citrus groves to the Pacific. On the

ABOVE: Aline Barnsdall "Hollyhock House" (Los Angeles, California, 1917). The poured-concrete house is as monolithic as a Mayan temple. The hollyhock - Barnsdall's favorite flower - theme runs through the house and the stylized hollyhock motif is repeated on stucco pinnacles on the exterior. In 1927 Aline Barnsdall gave the house and its grounds to the City of Los Angeles, and it is now a public park.

slopes of the hill Barnsdall planned for a theater and a
number of smaller buildings to be used as rehearsal and
dance studios, as well as apartments and retail units to
serve a Los Angeles community of avant-garde artists.

Although Wright knew that the Imperial Hotel project
would mean extended absences from America and that

185

Mrs. Barnsdall was a difficult client who would be unlikely to settle for dealing with his project supervisor - even if that supervisor were his own son - Wright, nevertheless accepted the commission.

The "Hollyhock House," a large and expensive complex, appears at first sight to be a monolithic concrete building. In fact its structure is not of concrete but of hollow clay tiles covered in stucco. The block-like simplicity is relieved only by the use of abstract patterns in the form of the stylized hollyhock motif. The main public rooms - entrance loggia, living room, music room and library - are organized in a T-shape, a device Wright had used frequently in many Midwestern Prairie Houses of the early 20th century. The "Hollyhock House," however, has two extended wings housing bedrooms and nursery in one, kitchen, dining room and servants' rooms in the other. The living room is dominated by the central fireplace with a decorative overmantle and projecting hearth surrounded by a pool of water. The large sculptural forms of the seating group - also designed by Wright - create an intimate space within the larger space of the room. Barnsdall's desire for a building that was half house and half garden was provided for in the numerous terraces, colonnades and pergolas that link the interior spaces with the gardens. The two wings enclose a garden court and, as in the

Robie House, entry to the "Hollyhock House" is complex: one enters from the side through the long entry loggia.

The "Hollyhock House," two guest houses and a spring house were the only structures completed in the lengthy building program. A fourth structure, known as the "Little Dipper" - a projected community playhouse - was begun but never completed. The "Little Dipper" was intended as a private school for Barnsdall's daughter, Betty, but it was also to be open to local children who would pay for their tuition.

Barnsdall's peripatetic lifestyle, and annoyance and disappointment at a house too large and at an expense too great, eventually led to her abandoning the main residence in favor of one of the smaller, Wright-designed buildings on the site. "Hollyhock House" illustrates Wright's long-term interest in primitive, non-European forms - particularly pre-Columbian architecture. His interest in Mayan architectural forms and in the decorative use of Mayan-inspired cast-concrete first manifested itself in the small warehouse built for Albert Dell German in Richland Center in 1915.

German was a wholesale commodities dealer who planned to expand his business, and he commissioned Wright to design a new warehouse. Wright conceived a four-story structure, whose brick walls rise from the

concrete base and are crowned by an intricate frieze in
contrasting gray concrete. Incorporated into the
geometric design of the frieze are 54 windows. The
reinforced concrete structure is designed with a grid of
massive concrete columns reinforced with steel and with
flaring capitals that carry the weight of the floor and the
roof. On the capitals of six of the columns, the motif of
the external frieze is repeated. The double brick wall skin
of the building created cold storage without the use of
mechanical refrigeration, while eliminating the interior
wall allowed for maximum internal storage space. In
addition to providing storage for German's wholesale
goods, the structure was also to contain a restaurant,
retail shopping units, an art gallery to display the works
of regional artists, and space dedicated to the display of
Wright's own handiwork.

The original construction costs were estimated at
$30,000, but by 1919 had escalated to $125,000 and in
1921 German was forced to halt the construction work.
In the 1930s he asked Wright to remodel the now
derelict interior, but financing proved impossible and

LEFT: A.D. *German Warehouse (Richland Center, Wisconsin, 1915).*
*An imposing cube reminiscent of Mayan architecture, this warehouse is
the only example of Wright's work in the town of his birth. The thick walls
of the building provided cold storage without mechanical refrigeration.*

German eventually lost the building through bankruptcy. The warehouse is still unfinished, but renovation in the 1980s provided a gift shop and small theater on the ground floor and an exhibition space featuring Wright's work on the second floor. It now houses the Richland Museum. Many recent commentators have remarked on the similarity of the warehouse's shape and appearance to the Mayan Temple of the Three Lintels in Chichen Itza in Yucatan.

Shortly after his arrival in Los Angeles, Wright began further experiments with concrete blocks, although at first he was mainly concerned with the massing and ornamental aspects of building with them, and not really with their structural system. However, he soon came up with the concept of the concrete textile-blocks. He hoped to devise an altogether new style of architecture, a key aspect of which would be the use of inexpensive concrete blocks that were very easy to manufacture and required only unskilled labor to erect. They were also easy to maintain, as they did not require any kind of exterior painting or need any protective coatings. In Wright's hands, these concrete blocks could in themselves provide interesting shapes and decorative patterned surfaces, and he spoke of this system as providing reasonably low cost housing to millions of Americans across the country.

For some time Wright had been trying to develop a concrete wall slab; to this end he and his son Lloyd Wright had been working on methods to link blocks together with steel rods that extended vertically and horizontally from one block to the next, to create a wall of any length and height. Two sets of linked blocks created the exterior and interior walls. Between the two walls was a hollow space, which allowed air to circulate, keeping the structure free of damp and the building cool in summer and warm in winter. The steel rods ran through channels along the top and sides of the blocks and, once fastened together, were sealed in place with concrete grouting. The result was a thin, but strong, reinforced slab wall. Because the wall could be made of blocks that were molded with a repeat pattern, Wright described himself as a "weaver" of what he called "textile" blocks.

The textile-blocks were first used in designs for the Doheny Ranch project, which never came to fruition, but the system was also indicated on drawings for two other houses in early 1923. One of these was designed for Aline Barnsdall for a site in Beverley Hills, as she was already thinking of quitting the "Hollyhock House," but, as with so many projects for this client, it was never built. The other was for the famous "La Miniatura," the Alice Millard House (1923). The sketches show two blocks formed to interlock with a hollow space between them and expanded metal is indicated for the assembly system. However, in the finished drawings for these two houses, the system is not worked out in any greater detail. It was only when the Millard House was restored and the walls were opened

that it was possible to see Wright's method of assembly - and discover that he had started from a concept different to the well-publicized one that followed.

RIGHT: *Alice Millard House "La Miniatura" (Pasadena, California, 1923). The first of Wright's textile-block designs, this house has a two-storey-high living room. Wright hoped that the textile-block houses would lead to a new style of American architecture, but problems with the construction technique were not fully resolved on these early projects.*

ABOVE: *The square blocks are patterned with a central sunken cross, which is reminiscent of the pre-Columbian architecture of Mitla, near Oaxaca in southern Mexico.*

There are two types of basic block: each is 15.5 inches square and they are assembled in pairs. The patterned blocks were used primarily for the exterior walls, and plain blocks used only in the interiors. Each block is designed to interlock: the patterned blocks have flanged edges that connect with semicircular cavities in the plain blocks. The blocks in the Millard House have no reinforcing metal rods but are laid with expanded metal on a conventional mortar bed.

"La Miniatura" was the first concrete block house to be built. Mrs. Millard had a limited budget, but Wright was eager to try his new system and he agreed to design the house without charging his standard fee, although he reserved an interest in the building in the form of a lien. He and Mrs. Millard signed a contract stipulating that Wright would be compensated in the event that the Millard House was sold speculatively for a profit.

Mrs. Millard had already purchased a treeless plot in Pasadena, but nearby she and Wright discovered a ravine in which stood two eucalyptus trees. However, the ravine was in fact an arroyo: dry for much of the year, in rainy seasons arroyos carry vast quantities of floodwater. Because of the amount and speed of flow of the water through these arroyos, they are much more dangerous to live by than the more harmless ravines of the Midwest. Flying in the face of wisdom, Wright decided to build the Millard residence at the bottom of the arroyo, so Mrs. Millard sold her original plot of land and bought the arroyo land - at an unsurprisingly cheap price!

The narrowness of the arroyo precluded the horizontal format of the Prairie House, and the textile block design was based on multiples of cubes, so the Millard House is a box. The north side of the house is placed next to a small lane and the visitor enters through a paved court leading to an entrance covered by a low bridge that spans from the house to the roof terrace over the attached garage. Inside, the two-story living room has a high window wall composed of glass doors at the lower level and a pattern of perforated concrete blocks set with glass above. The square blocks of which the house is constructed are patterned with a central sunken cross, which is reminiscent of the pre-Columbian architecture of Mitla, near Oaxaca in southern Mexico. Wright originally designed a studio addition to the southwest of the main house; this was carried out in 1926 by his son, Lloyd, who also doubled the size of the garage to hold two cars.

Like many of Wright's clients, Mrs. Millard was delighted with the design of the house and it was only during construction that the troubles began. A Pasadena building constructor, A.C. Parlee, agreed to build the house for $9,810 and the plans were agreed in March

ABOVE: *Samuel Freeman House (Los Angeles, California, 1923). In the textile-block houses, the precast concrete blocks were bound together on site with steel rods and poured concrete. The decorative patterned surface did away with the need for traditional plastering and paint finishes.*

196

1923, with work to be complete by October 1 - but the experimental nature of the block system caused delays. Although in concept the construction was simple, more than one type of block was required - perforated patterned blocks, half blocks, quarter blocks, corner blocks, and the 8 by 16 inch rectangular blocks that are stacked in single vertical rows to frame the windows and doors and form the piers at the entrance. Wright insisted that sand from the actual site be used for the concrete mix, his argument being that the color and texture of the concrete would be indigenous to the site. However, this "organic" approach had a major drawback: it was impossible to remove the impurities from the local sand, so the blocks proved unstable over time. In addition, the wooden molds for the blocks were made on site by Parlee's carpenter; one of these survives today and it is apparent that they were not precision-made so the blocks produced were never uniform in size.

In January 1924, with work on the Millard House half-finished, Parlee resigned from the project. In June he filed suit against Mrs. Millard, claiming more than $12,000 compensation for additional work he said he had carried out because changes had been made to the original plans - he claimed that these had originally called for a single rather than double-block wall construction. Mrs. Millard testified that this had never been so, and he lost the case. Rather than see this first experiment in textile-block remain unfinished, Wright himself contributed $6,000 to its construction costs and the house was eventually completed in 1924.

This was not the end of Mrs. Millard's problems though - the decision to site the house at the foot of the arroyo soon had repercussions. The culvert that had taken street water away below the basement level of the house for 50 years now overflowed and rose to the level of the dining room, burying the floors under layers of mud. The house was cleaned up with the help of the Pasadena City authorities, but Wright still had to sort out the problem of a leaking roof.

Several months after "La Miniatura" was started, Wright altered the method of concrete block construction: henceforth the blocks were held together by a network of internal joints filled with concrete grouting and steel reinforcing rods. By eliminating the mortar joints, Wright could also do away with skilled labor, while the addition of steel increased the structural and formal capabilities of the blocks - concrete works by

RIGHT: *Samuel Freeman House (Los Angeles, California, 1923). The last and smallest of the textile-block houses, built in the foothills of the Santa Monica Mountains. Its construction was supervised by Wright's son, Lloyd Wright, who also landscaped the site.*

compression, but by adding steel reinforcement it gains in tensile strength. Around the same time, Wright began the process of securing a patent on his new invention. On the next textile block house, the John Storer House (1923-24), the blocks were formed under pressure in machine-made metal molds, which were more precise. The blocks were then removed for the molds and allowed to dry for 10 days.

The youngest and possibly the least affluent of Wright's southern Californian clients were the Freemans. Samuel was a jewelery salesman and Harriet was interested in modern dance, and their building site was a small and steeply sloping plot in the Hollywood Hills. Its major feature was its view - below the site lay all of Hollywood. At approximately 120 square feet, the Freeman House was the smallest of the concrete-block houses, but also one of the most adventurous.

Responding to the needs of the Freemans and to the

LEFT: *Richard Lloyd Jones House (Tulsa, Oklahoma, 1929). There is little ornament in the Jones House. Concrete piers alternate with panels of glass and the severe design gives the building a fortress-like appearance.*

FOLLOWING PAGE: *The Jones House is two stories high for one third of its plan, and encloses a raised inner courtyard with a pool. It has six bedrooms, and also includes a library and a billiard room.*

RIGHT AND BELOW: *Erling P. Brauner House (Okemos, Michigan, 1948). A single-story adaptation of the Usonian House, the Brauner House is built in concrete block instead of brick. It is situated close to the Edwards House in Arrow Head Road.*

small site, Wright designed a concrete-block dwelling that was filled with light; it was airy and - in a manner not usually associated with concrete - it was very "delicate." The house was turned away from the street, opening it to the view: the front elevation is essentially a blank wall, while the back is almost entirely glazed. The plan is on two levels, with the living room and kitchen above and two bedrooms and a bathroom below. Placed on the extreme boundary of the site, Wright took advantage of an extra wedge-shaped area of land to site the garage. Once again the contract between the Freemans and Wright stipulated the cost - $9,100 - and a second agreement appointed Lloyd Wright as contractor. A final clause is reminiscent of the agreement with Alice Millard: if the Freeman House came

in at a cost greater than $10,000, Wright agreed to finance the completion of the work and would be reimbursed if the property were subsequently sold.

Once again, problems in construction appeared after the building had been started. There was a discrepancy in the land survey, so Wright had to alter parts of his original design: in turn this forced up the costs of the labor. However, the Freeman House is one of the most beautiful of Wright's buildings. The abundant use of perforated blocks, often set with glass, and the breaking

of the corners of the building with glass openings help
suggest the intimacy of the interior. The metal mullions
of the windows, which follow the pattern of the
adjoining block walls, make the concrete walls appear

ABOVE: *Erling P. Brauner House (Okemos, Michigan, 1948). The low roof of the house extends down and across the driveway, creating a covered carport. The concrete blocks are pierced at high level and inset with glass, providing light to the interior but protecting privacy.*

Above: *Charles W. Ennis House (Los Angeles, California, 1923).
Wright's largest and most elaborate commission in pre-cast concrete
textile-block, the Ennis House commands spectacular views over the city.*

more like thin screens than heavy masonry walls. The
Freeman House also has the most adventurous of the
block patterns: it was designed to be constructed out of
a single patterned block combined with plain blocks.

There are both left-hand and right-hand versions of the square and chevron asymmetrically-patterned blocks, and sometimes they are turned upside down. Some commentators have described the pattern as an abstraction of the eucalyptus tree, although Wright never mentioned an organic interpretation. The house incorporates the open plan and the central hearth of the earlier Prairie Houses and exploits the ornamental potential of concrete blocks combined with traces of Mayan, Mogul, Japanese and European modernism. The Freemans lived in their home for more than 50 years, making only a few changes to the layout in 1928 and 1932. At one point they divorced, but both were so fond of the house that they continued to live there "separately together."

The last of the concrete block houses in California was built for Charles W. and Mabel Ennis, and was the largest and most elaborate of all Wright's realized designs in this medium. Charles and Mabel Ennis were the owners of a men's clothing store in Los Angeles. Their site was on a steep mound at the base of the Santa Monica Mountains, elevated enough to be clearly visible from the city below. Wright's plan was for two buildings - the main house and a chauffeur's apartment and garage - separated by a paved courtyard. Constructed of 16-inch square blocks joined by metal reinforcing rods, the Ennis House (1923) rises in stages from an enormous platform buttressed by a retaining wall. Unlike the compact and vertically oriented compositions of the Millard, Storer and Freeman Houses, the Ennis House has a more attenuated plan, with the principal rooms occupying the second level. The unifying element is on the north side of the house: the 100-foot long loggia which links the main rooms and sets them open to the views of the city below. The division of the façade into zones of smooth and patterned blocks is continued on the interior walls, while geometric patterns in the art glass recall earlier designs in Prairie Houses.

As was now a regular occurrence, construction was fraught with problems. The blocks were made from decomposed granite that had been dynamited from the site during excavations for the foundations. The aggregate was then passed over a screen of quarter-inch mesh and only the finer particles that fell through the screen were used for the blocks. By September 1924, Lloyd Wright was wiring his father that the south walls

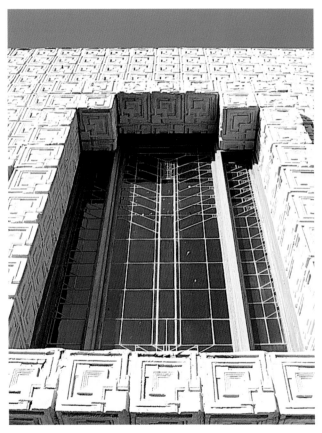

of the house were bulging and cracking and the lower blocks popping. The Ennises were becoming increasingly alarmed and eventually assumed control of the construction, carrying out several modifications - including adding several block courses to the lower walls and repositioning the front door. Inside the house, in addition to redesigned ceilings, a glass screen designed to separate the dining room from the loggia was not built and the low wall separating the dining room from the living room was reduced by one full block course. Other changes included the addition of an elaborate iron grillwork, a fireplace hood, chandeliers and the replacement of the specified shale paving in the entry and loggia by gleaming white marble. In 1940, the Ennis House was sold to radio personality John Nesbitt, who added a swimming pool and billiard room of Wright's design, but client and architect were soon at loggerheads and other work Nesbitt commissioned was never carried out.

After leaving California, Wright's first opportunity to exploit the textile-block system came when he was paid $10,000 for the rights to use it on the Arizona Biltmore

LEFT: *Charles W. Ennis House (Los Angeles, California, 1923). Detail of one of the windows of the Ennis House. The 16-inch square blocks are both structural and decorative.*

RIGHT: *Charles W Ennis House (Los Angeles, California, 1923). Detail of the art glass. Much of the glass was probably by Orlando Giannini, who had transferred his workshop from Chicago to California.*

Hotel in Phoenix, designed by architect Albert Chase McArthur. Wright stayed in Arizona for five months working closely with McArthur, but the extent of his involvement is unclear. During its construction, he was already busy with a new project - San Marcos in the Desert, a hotel suspended above the sloping site on cast concrete piers and supporting walls, which used the desert floor as their foundations. During experiments with the concrete, Wright and his entourage camped in the desert and his temporary home, named "Ocatillo" by his wife Olgivanna, appeared in several architectural magazines. The project was later abandoned, due to the Stock Market crash of October 1929.

There are a few other textile block houses, that were built after Wright left California. One was for his cousin, Richard Lloyd Jones in Oklahoma 1929; called "Westhope," most of it is a two-story building and it has an enclosed and raised inner courtyard with a swimming pool. The flat-roofed building was planned on a square grid and houses six bedrooms, a library, and a billiard room, as well as the usual dining room, living room, kitchen and servants' quarters. In 1948, Wright built a

Usonian House in Okemos, Michigan, for Erling P. Brauner, but using textile-blocks instead of brick, and in 1949 he built a single-story house for Eric V. Brown of textile block, overlooking Lake Lorenz.

RIGHT AND INSET: *Eric V. Brown (Kalamazoo, Michigan, 1949). This was one of four houses built by Frank Lloyd Wright at Parkwyn Village, although several more were designed in the original master plan. A single-story house overlooking Lake Lorenz, it was built from textile-block and mahogany and the living room has a terrace attached. The Browns were so eager to begin building their home that they arrived at Taliesin West with their children and announced they would wait for their drawings. They stayed for five days.*

THE USONIAN HOUSE

■ ■ ■

"Nature is my manifestation of God. I go to nature every day for inspiration in the day's work. I follow in building the principles which nature has used in its domain."

■ ■ ■

The 1930s were to be the years in which Wright produced some of his most accomplished works, including the famous house for Edgar Kaufmann, "Fallingwater." Yet one of Wright's most important contributions to architecture in these years was his solution to the problem of the small house with the development of the so-called Usonian House.

Between 1936 and 1941, when World War II virtually put a halt on all building except for military purposes, Usonian Houses sprang up all over the United States. The term Usonia is an acronym for the "United States of North America" - according to Wright the name came from Samuel Butler's novel Erewhon, although scholars have been unable to find the term used in that text.

LEFT: *Don & Virginia Lovness House (Stillwater, Minnesota, 1955). Interior of the Lovness House, showing some of the elegant furniture that was designed by Wright. The clients not only constructed their home, but also made all the custom-designed furnishings.*

ABOVE AND LEFT: *Kaufmann House "Fallingwater" (Bear Run, Pennsylvania, 1935).* One of the best-known Wright houses, Fallingwater is constructed of reinforced concrete slabs, cantilevered out from the rock and carrying the house over a stream and waterfall. From the square living room, a suspended stairway leads directly down to the stream, while immediately above terraces open out from the bedrooms. This house clearly illustrates Wright's view on architecture, which was poetic, romantic and intensely personal, and is one of the most spectacular designs of his mature period.

Whatever its origins, the idea of Usonia was Wright's key element in his response to the International Style of Le Corbusier and the like. For Wright, Usonia was an idealized location for which he could design a wide variety of building types, ranging from homes and farm buildings to gas stations and civic centers. Communities sometimes called Usonia I and Usonia II were planned for Lansing, Michigan and Pleasantville, New York. Only the last project was built - it was begun in 1947 - and then only the first three houses were designed by Wright. It was expected that local architects would complete the scheme - subject, of course, to his approval - since by this time Wright was well past his 80th birthday.

The cantilever feature of the Usonian House is nowhere better expressed than in Wright's most important and grand domestic commission of the 1930s, the house for Edgar J. and Liliane S. Kaufmann, "Fallingwater," the realization of Wright's romantic vision of man living in total harmony with nature. In 1934, Edgar J. Kaufmann Jr., partly as a result of reading Wright's autobiography, arrived at Taliesin. The son of a wealthy Pittsburgh department store owner, Kaufmann was to become an internationally famous historian and teacher. Visiting their son during his year-long stay at Taliesin, the senior Kaufmanns fell under Wright's spell.

ABOVE: *Kaufmann House "Fallingwater" (Bear Run, Pennsylvania, 1935). The feeling of nature is continued internally by the carrying the stonework inside on floors and walls, and by the use of almost uninterrupted glass, which offers outstanding views through the woods surrounding the house.*

Within a few months they asked him to design a new planetarium for Pittsburgh, which was never executed, a new office suite for Kaufmann at the department store, which is now housed in the Victoria & Albert Museum in London, and a country retreat for the Kaufmann family.

The Kaufmanns owned a tract of land, which

included a stream called Bear Run, in the mountains some 60 miles south of Pittsburgh; although the family used to camp on the site in summer, they now wanted a year-round house. Wright visited the site, noticed a large, smooth boulder overhanging a waterfall, and was told that Kaufmann liked to sunbathe there and that the whole family enjoyed swimming in the pools underneath the falls. Wright told his clients that he wanted them to "live with the waterfall" as an "integral part" of their lives. Consequently, he built the house directly over the stream and anchored it with a series of reinforced concrete "trays" attached to the masonry wall and natural rock forming the rear of the house. These trays cantilever over the falls, appearing to float weightlessly above the valley floor.

LEFT: *Kaufmann House "Fallingwater" (Bear Run, Pennsylvania, 1935). Fallingwater is a luxurious and beautiful testimony to Wright's genius. The inventiveness that Wright used in its design ensures that the building occupies a unique place in architectural history. The stone used in its construction is known as Pottsville sandstone.*

FOLLOWING PAGE: *Herbert Jacobs House I (Madison, Wisconsin, 1936). This is generally considered to be the first Usonian House to be built. Designed to an L-shaped plan, the construction materials of brick and redwood were typical of Usonian Houses.*

For the novel structural engineering this project required, Wright depended on his right-hand man, Wes Peters, and a Chicago engineer, Mendel Glickman. Rather than move the large boulder on which Kaufmann sunbathed, Wright incorporated it into the design so that it served as the hearth. Sandstone quarried on site, concrete and glass form the exterior and interior fabric of the building. The first-floor entry, the living room, and the dining room are integrated to form a continuous space. Dissolving the boundaries between interior and exterior space are walls of glass and wrap-around corner windows. A hatch opening to a suspended stairway allowed for ventilation and provided access to the stream below the house. The upper floors accommodate the bedrooms, which open onto private terraces.

"Fallingwater" became famous even before it was finished, with photographs appearing in newspapers around the world and a portrait of Wright on the cover of *Time* magazine. However, its construction was not without its problems - for a start, Kaufmann had envisaged that the house was to be located on the

RIGHT: *Herbert Jacobs House I (Madison, Wisconsin, 1936). Internally the red brick and three-inch redwood battens create a warm atmosphere. The house was so full of trend-setting ideas that Katherine Jacobs wrote a book about it.*

opposite side of Bear Run, where there was a splendid view of the waterfall, but Wright had placed it so that it was impossible to see the waterfall from the house. Kaufmann was also uneasy about having a house suspended in mid-air over a mountain stream and consulted an engineering firm who advised against going ahead with the scheme. Wright was so incensed that he demanded that work be stopped and his plans returned, but Kaufmann apologized and smoothed things over. Later another engineering firm suggested extending a wall by several feet to support one of the cantilevered terraces, which Kaufmann got the builders to do. When Wright discovered this he secretly had the top four inches of the wall removed, and then triumphantly showed Kaufmann that the terrace was supported exactly as he had designed it, and showed no signs of collapsing.

Although it has many Usonian features, "Fallingwater" was by no means a small or an inexpensive project. The Usonian House was intended to be low cost, and one of the first true examples was the first house for Herbert Jacobs in Madison, Wisconsin. Begun in 1936 and completed in 1938, the Jacobs House demonstrated Wright's complete rethinking of the small house. Herbert Jacobs, a journalist for the *Madison Capital Times*, and his wife Katherine had a small child and they were by no means wealthy, but they were both determined to have a house of distinction. Their ideal home was something in the Dutch Colonial style, but nothing like that was available in Madison and they were encouraged to seek out Wright instead. During their first meeting, Herbert Jacobs jokingly said that what America needed was a decent $5,000 house. Wright replied that he had been wanting to design a low cost house for 20 years, and that the Jacobs House could serve as a model for future commissions to be carried out on a larger scale.

Before the designs could be started, the Jacobs had to buy a plot of land. Although Wright suggested that they should consider the countryside, they opted for a suburban plot measuring only 60 feet by 120 feet - which used up much of their capital so the house itself would have to be financed by a mortgage. Wright wanted them to sell the plot and buy two on the other side of the street, and on that basis designed a house exactly 60 feet wide, which would not legally fit into the original land. On top of this, the Federal Housing Administration

FOLLOWING PAGE: *Herbert Jacobs House I (Madison, Wisconsin, 1936). The Jacobs were besieged by visitors so they started to charge 50¢ a time for tours – which they calculated would pay back the architect's fees by the time they came to sell the house.*

ABOVE: *Charles L. Manson House (Wausau, Wisconsin, 1938). This brick-built house is sheathed and partitioned by regular board-and-batten walls. A dropped ceiling in the children's bedrooms accommodates a second story, in a building barely higher than a single.*

refused the Jacobs a mortgage, because the flat roof of their house was against F.H.A. rules. In the end, a Madison banker who was a great fan of Wright's work lent them the $4,500 needed to build the house.

Wright exploited the small size of the site by turning the back of the house onto the street and organizing the building around an L-shaped courtyard. Inside, the main innovation was to abolish the dining room as a separate enclosed space. The kitchen is adjacent to the small dining area, so that Mrs. Jacobs could watch over her children playing outdoors, talk with her guests, and prepare, cook and serve a meal - all at the same time! The house gained almost instant public acclaim, largely because of its low cost at a time when America was emerging from the great depression, with many young couples wanting the opportunity to become owners of their own homes. Like all first examples, the Jacobs House had several flaws: the steam circulation heating system proved inadequate and was eventually replaced with a hot water system; storm windows and screens were later added to "weatherproof" the house.

The next Usonian House was built for Paul R. Hanna, a Stanford University academic, and his young family. However, the eventual size and cost - which greatly exceeded the budget of $15,000 - of the Hanna House was beyond the means of most Americans at the time. Nevertheless, the grid plan, the interior and exterior walls of board-and-batten construction, and the central

RIGHT: *Paul R. Hanna "Honeycomb House" (Stanford, California, 1936). Known as "Honeycomb House" because of its hexagonal module plan, this building was Wright's first in the Bay area of Stanford. The exterior walls are of brick, but many of the interior wooden walls were designed to be moveable so areas could be reconfigured as the children grew up.*

FOLLOWING PAGE: *The Hanna House is sited against a gently sloping hill, and terraces provide additional outdoor living space. It appears much more like an isolated country residence than the suburban house it is.*

location of the kitchen workspace are characteristics shared by all of the Usonian Houses. In this house Wright abandoned the square or rectangle as the basic unit for both the grid and plan in favor of a hexagon. This hexagonal plan gives the house its popular name, the "Honeycomb House." With walls joined at 120-degree angles, a fluid interior space and unrestricted views are created, further enhanced by the large amounts of glass that open out onto the brick terraces outside. The interior walls were designed so they could be moved and rearranged - when Hanna's children grew up, their section of the house was re-planned for the family's new needs.

The hexagonal module was used again in the Sidney Bazett House in 1939 and, as in the Hanna House, brick is used in the lower sections of the walls while the upper portions and the roof are in laminated redwood. Over the bedroom wing the roof is low and horizontal; inside, the spaces are small and feel more like ship's cabins. In contrast, the living/dining area, with its higher exposed gable roof, creates a more public space. The dining space projects out into one of the glass bays overlooking a terrace. In common with many Usonian Houses of the period, there is a long built-in couch next to the fireplace, above which - pierced through the laminated wood - is a long row of windows, through which natural light penetrates. Tucked behind the brick fireplace mass is the small kitchen.

Meanwhile, Wright was also working on Taliesin West in Arizona. In 1937, he had bought 600 acres of land in the Sonoran Desert at the foot of the McDowell Mountains, where he had established a second experimental "camp." Initially constructed in stone, cement, wood and canvas, the complex gradually altered and expanded, growing naturally out of the desert as the textures and colors of the building materials blended with the landscape. As the buildings became more permanent, steel and fiberglass was used to replace the less durable materials. The accommodation eventually included a drafting room, offices and studios, private living quarters, three theaters, a workshop and accommodation for fellows and staff, and it would serve as Wright's winter home, studio and "laboratory" of architectural ideas for the next 22 years. The living room at Taliesin West is dominated by the rugged masonry hearth and is framed by redwood forms that support the ceiling panels. The windows and hearth follow the triangular motif drawn from the shape of the surrounding mountains. The triangular shape is repeated again in the "origami" armchairs that appear as though they have been folded out of wood. At the heart of Taliesin West is the 96-foot by 36-foot drafting room,

BELOW: *Sidney Bazett House
(Hillsborough, California, 1939).
The Bazett House is Usonian in its use of
space, with the kitchen/workspace at the
center of the design. It was Wright's second
house in San Francisco and is of brick and
redwood batten, designed in hexagons.*

LEFT: *The living room projects into one of
the glass bays, while the kitchen is tucked
away behind a massive brick fireplace.
Essential to the idea of the Usonian House
was that furniture was largely unnecessary,
as much of it could be built into the walls.*

RIGHT: *Taliesin West (Scottsdale, Arizona, 1937-59). Wright's winter quarters began as an experimental camp in the desert but later evolved into a more permanent structure. Inside Taliesin West, the masonry and exposed beams are both structural and decorative. The furniture was all designed by Wright and is in keeping with his ideas about Usonian homes.*

FOLLOWING PAGE: *At Taliesin West, Wright conceived the desert rubblestone wall, which was created by placing large natural stones at random in forms and then pouring in concrete. The exposed faces of the stones were washed with acid to bring out their natural tones, and the buildings seem to "grow" out of the ground, blending with the natural colors and textures of the surrounding Sonoran Desert.*

a communal dining room and two apartments. Linking these core spaces is a terrace leading to the 56-foot long garden room with its sloping, translucent roof.

Before the United States entered World War II, Wright had designed and built numerous examples of the Usonian House across America, from California to New Jersey, and after the war the concept remained equally popular. In 1943, Wright wrote that the moderately priced house was not only America's major architectural problem but also the most difficult problem facing its major architects. For most of his remaining career, Wright was engaged in answering that problem, often through the Usonian House. An example is the Rosenbaum House (1939) in Alabama, a 1,540-square foot dwelling built at a cost of $12,000. In an attempt to design and construct simpler, more efficient houses suited to the informality of American family life, Wright eliminated the basement and attic, embedding the heating pipes in the concrete floor slab and placing the mechanical systems and the plumbing near the kitchen-workspace. His approach in many ways anticipated the prefabrication of many major building components: the walls, for example, were designed with an inner core of plywood that was sandwiched between board-and-batten interior and exterior surface walls. This did away with the need for traditional plaster and

ABOVE: Taliesin West (Scottsdale, Arizona, 1937-59). The drafting room at Taliesin West, showing the angular redwood forms of the roof - now covered in plastic.

FOLLOWING PAGE: Stanley Rosenbaum House (Florence, Alabama, 1939). An L-plan Usonian House, in which the basement and attics are eliminated and the heating pipes are embedded in the concrete floor mat. The walls consist of a plywood core sandwiched between the board-and-batten interior and exterior surfaces.

ABOVE: Stanley Rosenbaum House (Florence, Alabama, 1939).
This house is the only example of Wright's work in Alabama and it was renovated in 1970, when a Japanese garden was added.

FOLLOWING PAGE: The large living area opens off to the dining area and the kitchen. Wright also designed the built-in furniture in cypress wood for the room. It is complemented by carefully selected furniture from other leading designers - including the dining chairs by Charles Eames.

painted walls. Originally designed on an L-shaped plan on a two-foot by four-foot grid, the large living area included an asymmetrically placed hearth and dining area at one end, while at the other was a 100-foot long study area.

On the street side, the house appears as a nearly solid wall of Alabama clay and Southern cypress; reinforcing the overall horizontality of the building is the 20-foot long cantilevered carport. In contrast, the rear of the house has floor-to-ceiling windows, with doors opening onto the terrace and a Japanese garden, beyond which are woods.

Inside, fretwork wood panels frame clerestory windows and conceal the recessed lights. These are typical of Usonian Houses and articulate Wright's ideas about ornament being integral to the house. In his autobiography, Wright set down the design features he considered essential to the Usonian House. These ideas ranged from that of a visible roof being expensive and unnecessary, to furniture, pictures and bric-a-brac being unnecessary because the walls could be made to include them or even be them. In the Rosenbaum House, the Wright-designed furnishings are supplemented by pieces designed by Charles Eames.

Two other outstanding examples of the Usonian House of this period include the Pope-Leighey House

and the George D. Sturges House, "Skyeway," which dramatically cantilevers over its hillside site in Brentwood Heights, Los Angeles. The solidity of the brickwork on the entrance side of the building contrasts with the sense of lightness of the deck, balustrade and row of glass doors on the street side.

For Washington journalist Loren Pope and his wife, Wright designed a 1,200-square foot house for a cost of $7,000. Because of the design's radical nature, Pope could not get a mortgage - financing in the end came from his employer, *The Washington Evening Star* - and hired a builder who refused to sign a contract. As in most other Usonian Houses, the Pope-Leighey House (1939) is

ABOVE: *George D. Sturges House (Los Angeles, California, 1939). Constructed of brick and wood siding, this house is rather alarmingly cantilevered out from a hillside. The whole east side of the house opens out onto a balcony.*

modest in scale, has a flat roof with cantilevered car port, a heated concrete floor slab, recessed lighting, and uniform treatment of interior and exterior walls. The house was completed with plywood furniture built to Wright's specifications by Pope and the builder. In 1963, the house was earmarked for demolition by the Virginia State Highway Commission. The house's second owner, Mrs. Robert Leighey, donated the building to the National Trust for Historic Preservation, who dismantled it and moved it 15 miles from its site in Falls Church to a similar wooded hilltop on the Woodlawn Plantation.

During World War II there was little opportunity for building, but Wright was busy with plans for projects. The Lowell Walter House was first designed in 1942, although construction was delayed until 1945. The main house is a Usonian I-plan brick and steel construction, with the garden/living room turned to give better views

ABOVE RIGHT: *George D. Sturges House (Los Angeles, California, 1939). Known as "Skyeway," the Sturges House is an outstanding example of the Usonian House of this period. The solidity of the brickwork on the entrance side of the building contrasts with the sense of lightness of the deck, balustrade and row of glass doors on the street side.*

RIGHT: *The warm tones of the woodwork in the living room are very typical of Wright's interiors and give the room a very welcoming feel.*

258

LEFT: Loren Pope House (Falls Church, Virginia, 1939). The living room has modular plywood seating, which can be placed in a variety of configurations depending on the occasion. The interior space of the house, as with the other Usonian Houses, is designed for maximum flexibility. The other typically Usonian feature is the row of high clerestory windows, seen at the right, which admit light and at the same time allow a changing view of the top of the trees outside.

261

of the Wapsipincon River. Later Wright also designed a River Pavilion (1948), a brick boathouse that was sited further down the hill on the river, with a sun terrace and room above.

By now the Jacobs had outgrown their first house, and during the war years they came to him for a new design. The Jacobs House II (1944) is a two-story building planned in a semi-circle, set with its back into the ground of a hillside and facing south. Entry is via a tunnel through the wall of earth, and the living/dining room has a glass façade opening onto a sunken terrace. Again this new house was intended to be inexpensive to construct and Wright called it a solar hemicycle. Further

ABOVE: *Loren Pope House (Falls Church, Virginia, 1939). This building is now usually known as the Pope-Leighey House, after the second owner, Mrs. Robert Leighey, donated the building to the National Trust for Historic Preservation in 1963. It is a Usonian House with a typical horizontal, cypress-batten, dry-wall construction, around a brick core.*

LEFT: *Detail of the pierced wood panels in the Pope-Leighey House. It was moved from Falls Church to Mount Vernon to make way for a new interstate highway, but unfortunately it was rather unsympathetically sited in its new location.*

examples are the Ken Laurent House (1949), and the Curtis Meyer House (1948). The Laurent House is a single-story Usonian solar hemicycle, constructed from common brick and cypress. The plan incorporated special access facilities for the disabled owner. The Meyer House (1948) is an east-facing solar hemicycle built from concrete block. When the end of the war came in 1945, Wright was already 78 years old. However, at an age when most people are slowing down, he was gearing up to a new period of activity.

While most of the small domestic commissions of the post-war period were carried out under Wright's supervision by senior members of the Taliesin

PREVIOUS PAGE: *Lowell Walter House (Quasqueton, Iowa, 1945). The pierced roof and huge windows of the garden/living room allow enough light to sustain a flourishing interior garden. The windows also give extensive views of the river below.*

RIGHT: *The main house is a Usonian I-plan in brick and steel, with the garden/living room turned to give better views of the Wapsipinicon River. It is a derivative of the "glass house" that appeared in the Ladies' Home Journal. Wright called it his "Opus 497" - the number of houses he reckoned to have produced by 1945. Further down the hill, on the banks of the river, is the River Pavilion, a brick boathouse with a sun terrace and a room above. Restoration work was carried out in 1991.*

ABOVE AND LEFT: *Herbert Jacobs House II (Middleton, Wisconsin, 1944). The second house that Wright built for Jacobs is a two-story, solar hemicycle house, with its back set into the ground and a glass façade to the front opening onto a sunken terrace. Entry is via a tunnel that runs through the wall of earth.*

269

ABOVE: *Kenneth Laurent House (Rockford, Illinois, 1949). A single-story Usonian solar hemicycle, this house is constructed from common brick and cypress. The plan incorporates special access facilities for its original owner, who was disabled.*

LEFT: *The living room opens out onto a slope, which leads down to Spring Creek. The hemicycle concept reflects Wright's growing fascination with circular forms.*

Fellowship, occasionally Wright took a particular interest in a house whose site had caught his attention. This was the case with the house on a rocky stretch of beach at Carmel for Mrs. Clinton Walker. Situated overlooking Monterey Bay, the house has a "floating" blue-colored metal roof. In keeping with the coastal theme, the pointed prow-like form of the stone terrace makes the house look remarkably like a boat about to put out to sea. Wright used a variation on the Usonian plan, with the living/dining room organized around a fireplace, and a kitchen core, off which a galleried wing contained three bedrooms and baths. The plan is based on a module of four-foot interlocking equilateral triangles, put together rather like a jigsaw puzzle. An almost unbroken band of casement windows provides views across the ocean and, ingeniously, the horizontal mullions of the windows are corbelled one above the other to allow sections of the windows to be opened downwards, rather than outwards, thus stopping winds and sea spray being blown into the house.

In design, the house for Robert Berger (1950) in San

ABOVE AND RIGHT: *Curtis Meyer House (Kalamazoo, Michigan, 1948).*
Built in the housing development of Galesberg Country Homes, this solar
hemicyle house faces east and is built from concrete block. The development
was conceived by a group of chemists working at a company in Kalamazoo,
and Wright designed four of the houses in 1948 - the Meyer House, the
Eppstein House, the Pratt House and the Weisblatt House.

RIGHT: Mrs. Clinton Walker House (Carmel, California, 1948). A Usonian House of stone, rising from a rocky promontory on the beachfront and looking out over Monterey Bay. The blue-colored metal living room roof is cantilevered away from the masonry core so that no weight rests on the stepped bands of glass facing the ocean. The almost unbroken band of casement windows provides views across the ocean and because the horizontal mullions of the windows are corbelled one above the other, sections of the windows can be opened downwards, rather than outwards, thus stopping winds and sea spray being blown into the house.

LEFT: *The pointed prow-like form of the stone terrace makes the house look remarkably like a boat about to put out to sea.*

FOLLOWING PAGE: *Robert Berger House (San Anselmo, California, 1950). A Usonian House of one storey, the Berger House is constructed of rubblestone and wood.*

ABOVE: *Robert Berger House (San Anselmo, California, 1950). Set into the steep slope of a hillside, the house reworks the 1930s Usonian House and was built by Berger himself. The low-pitched roof extends over the rubblestone walls of the house.*

280

Anselmo, California, reworks the 1930s Usonian House. The fireplace and kitchen workspace make up the central masonry core. Off to one side is the living room, to the other is the bedroom wing. Outside, the low-pitched roof extends over the rubblestone and glass walls of the house, which is set into the steep slopes of the hillside. Extending from the living room is a concrete and stone parapeted terrace in the form of a ship's prow.

In the Zimmerman House (1950) in New Hampshire, brick, cast

FOLLOWING PAGE: *William Palmer House (Ann Arbor, Michigan, 1950). This single-story Usonian House was built for a Professor of Mathematics at the University of Michigan. It has a triangular plan, which perfectly complements the hilltop on which it rests.*

concrete and cypress are used to create a house that is sited diagonally on a one-acre plot. The street façade is dominated by a solid masonry wall pierced by a high, continuous band of windows. In contrast, the garden façade is made of floor-to-ceiling glass, mitered at the corners. In addition to the house, Wright also designed the landscape, all of the free standing and built-in furniture, and he even selected the textiles and family's tableware. The internal organization of space, with variations in ceiling height, the use of built-in furniture and the continuous concrete floor slab make the Zimmerman House appear much larger than its actual 1,458 square feet. When the Zimmermans first contacted Wright they had expressed their wish for a house that was an expression of their personal way of

ABOVE: William Palmer House (Ann Arbor, Michigan, 1950). Although the house is mainly built of brick, a row of brick-colored, pierced concrete blocks has been incorporated into the outside walls, which both add texture to the exterior and introduce extra light to the interior. The changing levels and roofline also introduces extra layers of visual interest to the design of the building.

LEFT: *Zimmerman House (Manchester, New Hampshire, 1950). One of only two examples of Wright's work in New Hampshire, the Zimmerman House is a single-story building with clerestory windows providing additional light in the garden/living room.*

FAR LEFT INSET: *The large garden/living room originally doubled as a concert space, and opens onto a terrace and landscaped garden beyond. It was accommodated in the rather modest building by making all the other rooms relatively small in size.*

LEFT INSET: *Detail of the pierced concrete blocks set with glass that provide extra light to the living room.*

287

life and Wright responded with the design that he called a "classic Usonian." In 1952, the Zimmermans wrote again to Wright, telling him that their house "was the most beautiful house in the world."

The Kalil House (1955) in Manchester, New Hampshire, draws on elements that Wright used in the Californian cast-concrete houses of the 1920s. The main part of the house is built on an L-shaped plan, which is extended into a T-shape by the addition of a carport. Also in 1955 was the Lovness House in Stillwater, Minnesota, built for Don and Virginia Lovness. They constructed their own home and made all the custom-designed furnishings. The main building is of local

PREVIOUS PAGE: *Zimmerman House (Manchester, New Hampshire, 1950). A long structure of red-glazed brick, Georgia cypress trim and flat terracotta roof tiling, the Zimmerman House is set in a wooded garden and has a warm and inviting appearance.*

ABOVE LEFT AND LEFT: *Toufic H. Kalil House (Manchester, New Hampshire, 1955). This Usonian "automatic" House is built to an L-plan, extended into a T with the addition of a carport on one side. There are no large windows anywhere in the building - light is admitted only through the pierced and glazed concrete blocks, which are used structurally as in the textile-block houses. The building has a rather fortress-like appearance, in strange contrast to its setting amidst woodland.*

PREVIOUS PAGE: Don & Virginia Lovness House (Stillwater, Minnesota, 1955). This single-story structure is one of the last Usonian Houses. It is constructed from stone and wood and the master and guest bedrooms form separate wings to the main building. The elegant furniture was designed specifically for the building.

ABOVE RIGHT: The building blends extremely well with its setting, and the windowed walls offer outstanding views of the surrounding woodland. The stone used in its construction is Dolomite, a local hard limestone.

RIGHT: The house is a small treasury of Wright design, both in its construction and in the interior fittings and furniture. Wright also designed a small one-room cottage for Lovness, also in Stillwater, Minnesota, in 1958.

ABOVE: *Dorothy Turkel House (Detroit, Michigan, 1955). The only two-story, Usonian "automatic" House is built on an L-plan with a double-height living room. There are no large windows in the building - but more than enough light is admitted through floor-to-ceiling pierced and glazed concrete blocks.*

RIGHT: *Detail of one of the exterior walls of the Turkel House.*

RIGHT: *George Ablin House* (*Bakersfield, California, 1958*).
The use of concrete blocks is managed in a very interesting way in the
George Ablin House. The contrast between the large south-facing dining
room of glass and wood and the poolside main construction of salmon
concrete block - some perforated to provide windows - is very striking.

BELOW RIGHT: *Pierced concrete blocks set with glass form the masonry*
core housing the kitchen area.

limestone - known as Dolomite - and wood, with the
master bedroom and guest bedrooms forming the
separate wings.

A late Californian house for George C. Ablin from
1958 also uses the triangular module. The pink walls of
this house are concrete block and include patterned
perforated blocks as windows. The low-pitched, wood
shingled, gable roofs extend outwards to provide shade
for the glass walls, terraces and the entry walk. Leading
to the central core of entry room, living room, dining
room and high-ceilinged kitchen is a covered walkway.
From the central core two wings extend, housing
bedrooms and a study in one, and a children's playroom
and bedrooms in the other. Inside, the house is
furnished with examples of Wright's free standing
wooden furniture.

In the post-war years, Wright frequently elaborated

on his theme of the Usonian House. Though always arranged around a tight, compact masonry core, the houses were often enlarged and loosely spread out over their sites.

RIGHT AND BELOW: *Willard H. Keland House (Wisconsin, 1954). Willard H. Keland was married to Karen Johnson, the daughter of the owner of Johnson Wax. He was first president of the corporation that built the Riverview Terrace Restaurant. Their house had additions made to it by John H. Howe in 1961. Wright designed several buildings for the Johnson family, including the fabulous "Wingspread."*

Religious Buildings

■ ■ ■

"Form follows function - that has been misunderstood.
Form and function should be one, joined in a spiritual union."

■ ■ ■

It was from his mother's family that Frank Lloyd Wright acquired his religious and philosophical outlook. The Lloyd Joneses had a tradition of religious dissent that mixed Unitarianism and Welsh non-conformist beliefs with the intellectualism of the New England Transcendentalists into a form of Protestantism that was suspicious of any orthodox religion that interfered with the individual's quest for spiritual truth. Wright's own commitment to Unitarianism, and to the principles of spiritual unity it promoted, continued throughout his life and one of his first large public buildings was the Unity Temple, designed 1904 and built in 1905-08 for the Unitarian congregation of Oak Park, Illinois.

At the beginning of June 1904, the wooden frame

LEFT: *Unity Temple (Oak Park, Wisconsin, 1904). One of the 17 buildings listed by the A.I.A., the Unity Temple is considered to be the first significant American building to use poured concrete - which was in part dictated by the need to keep cost down.*

church of the Unitarian congregation in Oak Park had burnt down. Although Wright had been a member of the congregation for many years, it was surprising that the pastor, Dr. Johonnot, awarded him the commission to design a replacement, as Johonnot was not considered progressive in his taste. His vision for the new church was for a New England style meeting house with a tall spire; what he got was a concrete structure with a cantilever roof. Original Wright plans had specified brick and stone, but it seems that the potential offered by concrete - the medium he was using in the E-Z Factory at the time - was irresistible. Furthermore, congregational funds for the new building were restricted and so fine masonry and other materials were simply beyond the budget. For $35,000 Wright had to provide a church with an auditorium and

RIGHT: *Unity Temple (Oak Park, Wisconsin, 1904). The simple exterior forms were embellished with cast-concrete decorative details and the church itself contains a number of innovative features - including highly sophisticated hot air circulation.*

parish house, for a congregation that numbered well over 400 people. Out of the funds also had to come the cost of materials and the cost of labor. One of the main causes of the delays in the construction of the building was the simple fact that the workers employed on the project were not familiar with the techniques of building in this new material, and many of them disapproved wholeheartedly of its use for anything other than factory buildings.

The exterior of the church is a monolithic mass of concrete. The walls, with their rough surface, were left undressed, exactly as they emerged from their wooden molds into which the

LEFT: *Unity Temple (Oak Park, Wisconsin, 1904). The plan of the interior is a Greek cross inscribed within a square and ceiling is highest over the central area. In the four short arms the ceiling is lower, with banks of windows at the top. Although it is severe on the outside, inside the Temple is richly decorated with art-glass and wood trim and Wright called it "my little jewel box."*

concrete was poured and in which it dried. Over time, the surfaces have weathered down to a golden hue and in parts vines and creepers have grown, softening the building's appearance. The impression that the viewer receives - inside and out - is that they are looking at an arrangement of Froebel's kindergarten "Gifts" - building blocks arranged on top of and next to each other. The plan of the cube containing the auditorium is a Greek cross inscribed in a square and the space inside it is filled with different levels of seating. Over the center of the cross, the ceiling reaches its highest point with a skylight above. The four short arms of the cross have slightly lower ceilings and have banks of windows at the top. Placed between the arms of the cross are stair towers whose roofs are lower still. Unity Temple not only marked a definite break with traditional ecclesiastical architecture, but it was a pioneer American building in reinforced concrete. With this building, Wright became the first architect of modern times to use a completely new imagery to describe the relationship between God and man.

During World War II, one of Frank Lloyd Wright's major commissions was for the Community Church (1940) in Kansas City, Missouri. The building he planned for the congregation of Dr. Burris A. Jenkins was to be a "church of the future," but financial constraints, wartime shortages of materials and restrictive building codes greatly compromised the design. As originally planned, this building was the first drive-in church, but the scheme for the parking terraces had to be abandoned, as did the rooftop gardens, and consequently Wright considered the building to be his in shape only and refused to list it among his completed works.

For the plan, Wright used a rhombus with two 120-degree angles and two 60-degree angles as the basic unit for the design. Instead of the "traditional" concrete structure, Gunite - an inexpensive, strong yet lightweight and fireproof concrete material - was sprayed over sheets of corrugated steel which were then sandwiched together to form the walls. This method allowed the walls to be reduced in thickness to a mere 2.75 inches and furthermore it was cheap and fast. The new church was being built because the old one had burned down so the congregation was presently homeless: to build a church from brick or stone would take time and a considerable amount of money which would have to be raised. Wright promised Dr. Jenkins a church for $150,000 and, as usual, almost immediately there were problems. Local builders were reluctant to bid on the project, the local authorities refused a building permit - their codes demanded poured concrete foundations and not Wright's proposed rock ballast ones - until Wright finally

FRANK LLOYD WRIGHT

PREVIOUS PAGE: *Community Church (Kansas City, Missouri, 1940). There were problems during the construction of this church - mainly due to differences of opinion between Wright and his client. Wright wanted to use pressure-sprayed concrete, but was overruled.*

RIGHT: *Detail of Wright's free standing metal sculpture for the exterior of the Community Church, based on intersecting cross forms. Unfortunately wartime restrictions on finances and materials severely compromised Wright's original plans.*

FAR RIGHT: *The domed roof of the hexagonal chancel is perforated and powerful searchlights with a combined illumination power of 1.2 million candles create a dramatic "steeple of light," which reaches several miles into the sky.*

312

gave up on the project and any hope of his fees.

A perforated dome was constructed to roof the hexagonal chapel, but the searchlights that Wright had envisaged to create the "Steeple of Light" were not installed until 1994. On weekends and holidays, the lights - with their combined illumination power of 1.2 million candles - project through the pierced dome and reach several miles into the sky.

In the 1938, Wright had formally joined the First Unitarian Society in Madison, Wisconsin and just under 10 years later he designed its famous meeting house. Commissioned in 1946, the Unitarian Meeting House - which Wright described as a hilltop "country church" took five years to build and exceeded by three and a half times the initial budget of $60,000 - even though most of the labor came from the volunteer workforce of the congregation itself. Constructed of more than 1,000 tons of rough cut limestone, the congregation carted the building materials from a quarry 30 miles away. For the plans Wright accepted a minimal fee, offered the assistance of the Taliesin fellows and apprentices and also helped to raise funds for the construction by giving two lectures.

The design of the meeting house is based on a diamond module and the geometric form is repeated in the incised pattern on the concrete floor. The meeting house, however, is dominated by the steep, prow-like roof of welted copper that rises to a pointed gable over the pulpit and choir loft - which proved to be too small for a choir of any decent size and now houses the organ pipes. The auditorium and adjacent hearth room can, by contrast, accommodate 340 people and a loggia leads to the west living room where social functions are held. For both the auditorium and hearth room Wright designed collapsible benches and tables. At the meeting house's dedication in August 1951 he gave an address on "Architecture as Religion" from the pulpit of the church - whose roof he described as "hands joined in prayer."

In the design of the Beth Sholom Synagogue (1954-59) in Elkins Park, Pennsylvania, Wright intended the building to symbolize the rock from which Moses descended with the Ten Commandments. Entering the synagogue, worshipers could feel as though they had entered a light-filled crystal at whose metaphorical center was the holy word of God. The complex symbolism of the synagogue was the result of close

PREVIOUS PAGE: *Unitarian Meeting House (Shorewood Hills, Wisconsin, 1946). Wright was active in fund-raising for this church and he was even more deeply involved than usual with the design. The interior has an atmosphere of calm and reverence that is conducive to quiet worship.*

LEFT: *Built in limestone and oak, the Meeting House originally had a plan formed of two conjoined triangles of different sizes, with side wings for the Sunday school and facilities, but an additional wing was added by Taliesin Architects after Wright's death.*

collaboration with the commissioner, Rabbi Mortimer J. Cohen - so much so that Wright's initial sketches bore Cohen's name as co-designer. When Cohen had been informed that the congregation was prepared to raise half a million dollars for a new synagogue, he had set down in sketches exactly what the ideal synagogue should be. First, there was to be no reference to any earlier architectural styles and, second, he wanted the synagogue

RIGHT: *Beth Sholom Synagogue (Elkins Park, Pennsylvania, 1954). The tripod-shaped synagogue was dedicated on September 20, 1959. A huge, translucent form, roofed in glass, the building is suspended from a tripod frame, so that a full upper floor, directly above the chapel below, is completely free of any internal supports.*

ABOVE: Beth Sholom Synagogue (Elkins Park, Pennsylvania, 1954).
Detail of the roof. The synagogue is constructed from concrete, steel,
aluminium, glass, fiberglass and oiled walnut.

FOLLOWING PAGE: Beth Sholom Synagogue (Elkins Park, Pennsylvania,
1954). The translucent, pyramidal shape of the synagogue is very
characteristic of Wright's daring approach to such commissions. The
triangular forms of the ground plan and structure are repeated in the
triangular design modules of the stained glass and other fixtures.

to be the embodiment of the idea of the Tabernacle that God had instructed Moses to build for the wandering Jews. Cohen was urged to contact Wright by his friend Boris Blai, who had taught at Florida Southern College in the 1940s and who had become a close friend of Frank Lloyd Wright. Cohen contacted Wright and sent him the sketch. Normally Wright would have rejected outright anyone who he believed simply wanted him to transform their own ideas into a building, but on this occasion he agreed to meet with the Rabbi to discuss the project.

The plans and elevations for the synagogue revealed that Wright had indeed translated Cohen's desire into a building: a tabernacle also implied tent, and Wright designed a building whose shape was certainly tent-like. Three huge steel and concrete uprights sheathed in copper - although later aluminium was substituted - rise 117 feet into the air and form a tripod from which sloping walls of translucent plastic hang. The tripod rests on a cradle of reinforced concrete, from which three wings spring out, reversing the angle to absorb the outward thrust of the tripod's legs. The structure's roughly hexagonal plan, according to Wright, mirrored the shape of cupped hands - the cupped hands of God, in which the congregation safely rests - while the ramps of broad, deep stairs with shallow risers leading from

the main entrance to the main sanctuary are intended to
suggest the ascent of Mount Sinai. The 100-foot high,
pyramidal, translucent roof thus takes on the form of the
mountain itself, and the light that filters through its
walls symbolizes the divine gift of the law. The main
sanctuary can accommodate 1,100 people in seating
arranged in triangular sections around two sides of the
projecting pulpit. The pulpit, or Bimah, by tradition is
the platform from which the rabbi and cantor conduct
the service and is generally in a low place, in the middle
of the auditorium of a synagogue. This tradition was not
strictly adhered to, as Wright argued that the lowest
point in the auditorium was needed for seats, and every
seat he could provide would pay for the synagogue. The
40-foot high concrete monolith that represents the
stone tablets given to Moses forms the backdrop to the
Ark containing the 10 Torah scrolls, one for each of the
commandments. Cohen had reminded Wright also that
the Ark had to be made of wood, because metal was
forbidden material as it was a symbol of war, and that it
must always be approached by steps - never fewer than
three steps and as many as 12, as in the ancient temple
in Jerusalem. Over the Ark, Wright had argued for a
representation of the Burning Bush as a feature of the
lighting. Cohen, however, was against the concept and
sent Wright his design for the triangular glass and

aluminium sculpture, "Wings," the colors of which symbolize divine emanations. In addition to the main sanctuary, the Beth Sholom Synagogue also has a smaller sanctuary that can accommodate 250 worshippers, lounges, offices and meeting rooms, all of which can be accessed from the main entrance.

By the time the Beth Sholom Synagogue was completed in 1956, Wright was busy at work on another religious building, the Annunciation Greek Orthodox Church (1956) in Wauwatosa, Wisconsin. In this building he incorporated the symbols of the Greek Orthodox faith in the plan, essentially a Greek cross circumscribed by a circle. The same device was translated into the decorative elements and appears throughout the sanctuary. Four equally-spaced reinforced concrete piers support the domed structure and define the cross on the main floor. Inside, the sanctuary has no interior supports to obstruct the view of the worshippers and no parishioner sits more than 60 feet from the sacristy. A lower level seats 240 people and also contains a circular banqueting hall connected to an underground classroom. Circular stairs lead to the upper level, which seats a further 560 congregants. Light enters the building through semicircular windows and 325 transparent glass spheres that separate the edge of the upper wall and the domed roof. The dome itself is of concrete, but is not fixed to the outer wall; it floats on a bed of thousands of steel bearings contained in the circular channel beam capping the outer wall. Originally the dome was covered in celestial-blue colored ceramic tiles, which were later replaced with a synthetic roofing material. The Annunciation Greek Orthodox Church took two years to complete and was dedicated in 1961.

The tent-like structure of the Beth Sholom was a form to which Wright returned in designs completed shortly before his death for the Pilgrim Congregational Church (1958) in Redding, California. In addition to the tent-like sanctuary, the project consisted of an adjacent chapel, church

RIGHT: *Annunciation Greek Orthodox Church (Wauwatosa, Wisconsin, 1956). The plan at the main level forms a Greek cross circumscribed by a circle; the same device was translated into decorative elements and appears throughout the sanctuary. Four concrete piers define the shape on the ground floor.*

PREVIOUS PAGE: Annunciation Greek Orthodox Church (Wauwatosa, Wisconsin, 1956). The dome is not fixed to the piers but floats on thousands of steel ball bearings inside the circular beam that caps the outer supporting wall. Light enters the building through semicircular windows and through 325 glass spheres that separate the outer wall and the domed roof.

ABOVE: Pilgrim Congregational Church (Redding, California, 1958).
Part of a much larger scheme, the remainder of which was abandoned
after Wright's death, the design of this church was based on a triangular
module symbolizing the Christian Trinity. This is evident in the details of
the interior, including the floor tiles and the ceiling.

ABOVE: *Pilgrim Congregational Church (Redding, California, 1958). The base of the structure is of desert rubblestone and triangular steel and concrete pillars support the building. The steel roof is suspended from rows of white concrete pylons, which make the structure look rather like a giant tent.*

offices, and a fellowship hall. The building structure has a rough-cut stone and concrete base, over which a metal

roof is suspended from rows of high-pitched pre-cast concrete supports - rather like tent poles. The plan is based on a triangular module, evident in the tiles of the floor and in the details of the wooden interior ceiling. Completed in 1963, the church still lacks the intended central stone tower surmounted by a thin metal spire that would have unified the structure's three main "wings."

COMMERCIAL AND
CIVIC COMMISSIONS

■ ■ ■

*"Classicism is a mask and does not reflect transition.
How can such a static expression allow interpretation of
human life as we know it? A firehouse should not resemble
a French chateau, a bank a Greek temple and a university
a Gothic cathedral. All of the isms are an imposition
on life itself by way of previous education."*

■ ■ ■

One of Wright's first commercial commissions was the
Larkin Company Administration Building (1903), and it
remains one of his most important works, even though it
was demolished in 1950. It not only represented a new
architectural form but was also a radical concept of what
an office should be, since Wright wished to introduce
the therapeutic value of space and light into an office
building. The Larkin Company was the world's largest
manufacturer of soaps, perfumes and toilet

LEFT: *Rookery Building remodeling (Chicago, Illinois, 1905). This
Chicago skyscraper was designed by another architect, but Frank Lloyd
Wright was commissioned to remodel the entrance area and lobby, which
have now been meticulously restored.*

preparations, which were sent directly from the factory to the home user without middlemen. As the goods were shipped by rail, the factories were situated by railway lines and - because trains were coal-powered - these sites were dark, dirty and noisy.

The plot earmarked for the new administration building was a trapezium-shaped area bordered on one side by the New York Central railroad line and on the other two sides by streets full of horse-drawn vehicles. In response, Wright conceived a plan that was totally sealed off from its surroundings, with a six and a half-story courtyard building as the main factory and a smaller annex to house most of the company's support activities. The main structure was based on an open plan, with a series of tall galleries located around a central, vertical court that was top-lit by rooflights. Around the exterior wall, windows provided additional light. The building was inward-looking, with a glass roofed central hall rising its full height with office floors encircling it. Wright not only designed the building but all the interiors and the office furniture - including a

RIGHT: *Rookery Building remodeling (Chicago, Illinois, 1905). View of the upper level of the lobby area. Wright had wanted to build a skyscraper for many years, but none of his tower projects was realized until the Price Company Tower in 1952.*

three-legged chair that was so unstable that it became known among Larkin employees as "the suicide chair." The Larkin building was designed to be fireproof, and also contained the first use of double glazing, modular steel and glass fittings, hanging bathroom partitions and wall-hung lavatories. All that remains of it today are fragments of the foundations, but Wright took some satisfaction in his autobiography in learning how difficult - and how expensive - it had been to demolish!

ABOVE: City National Bank (Mason City, Iowa, 1909). The bank and Park Inn Hotel behind it have been substantially altered - particularly by the insertion of shop windows at ground floor level. Brick piers with colored terracotta decoration frame the art-glass windows.

In 1905, after nearly a year's continuous absence from Chicago working on projects in Buffalo, New York, Wright came back to Illinois. His return was marked by a continuing interest in non-domestic projects - factories, retail shops and office interiors. In this period he designed the E-Z Polish Factory, the Pebbles and Balch Shop, Browne's Bookstore, the Thurber Art Gallery and redesigned the entrance lobby of the Rookery Building.

One of the largest of these non-domestic commissions was the City National Bank and Hotel, in Mason City, Iowa. This was begun in 1909, and the project was sponsored by the law firm of Blythe, Markley, Rule and Smith. Mr. Markley's daughters were pupils at the Hillside Home School and an accidental meeting between Wright and Markley at the Lloyd Jones's resulted in the commission. The law firm wanted a structure that would function as a civic center in which were the facilities of a bank, a hotel (to be known as the Park Inn and to be Wright's first venture in hotel design), and retail shops. In the plan of the building, Wright allowed the various functions of the elements to dictate the layout, resulting in an asymmetric composition of buildings that spread along a long axis. The two main areas, the bank with business offices above it and the hotel-cum-shopping building, are linked together by the lines of the heavily projecting roof slab.

By 1915, Wright had seen the Ho-o-den reconstruction at the World's Fair and also the reconstruction of the Mayan Nunnery at Uxmal. It sparked off an interest in Mayan architectural forms,

RIGHT: *A.D. German Warehouse (Wisconsin, 1915). The warehouse is very reminiscent of Mayan architecture - particularly in the design used for the cast-concrete blocks. Incorporated into the design of the frieze are 54 windows.*

FOLLOWING PAGE: *The lower part of the warehouse is of red brick and the top story is faced in finely patterned abstract geometric shapes, of cast-in-place concrete. Construction was halted in 1921, and the entrances blocked over, when German lost the property through bankruptcy.*

ABOVE: Arthur L. Richards Bungalow (Milwaukee, Wisconsin, 1916).
An example of the prefabricated bungalow that Wright designed for the
Richards Company. As a self-assembly home it retailed for as little as
$23,750, and there was also a single-story, flat-roofed house.

348

which manifested itself in the Mayan-inspired cast-concrete decoration on the A.D. German Warehouse (1915). How Wright came to be offered this commission is something of a mystery, although local legend has it that Wright owed German a substantial sum of money for supplies he had purchased over the years and had never paid for. He is therefore supposed to have volunteered the design of a new warehouse as a way of discharging the debt. The rather lump-like cube of the warehouse stands out in stark contrast to every other building in Richland Center, and many in the town must have struggled to see any beauty in it.

FOLLOWING PAGE: *Arthur L. Richards Duplex Apartments (Milwaukee, Wisconsin, 1916). These four separate buildings are all from the American System Ready-cut prefab plans of 1916. They each had upper and lower apartments, and were originally all surfaced in plaster with a wood trim.*

Some of the commercial projects that Wright designed also crossed over into the domestic area. In keeping with his general interest in the area of low cost housing, Wright also became involved with designing for manufacturers of pre-fabricated houses. As early as 1916, he designed a variety of dwellings for Arthur L. Richards' companies, known as the American System Ready-cut prefab plans. All of them were designed to be cut at the factory and shipped to site ready for construction. The plans were not only for single houses, but also for duplex apartments.

For the Marshall Erdman Company he came up with several different designs, but only two were built in reasonable numbers. The Carl Post House (1956) is an example of Pre-Fab No. 1 and is built on an L-shaped plan, with the kitchen and dining facilities in the shorter leg and the living room below the entrance at the inner intersection of the L. The building has a masonry core and is built of brick with horizontal board-and-batten siding on the bedroom wing. The Pre-Fab No. 2 was a square-plan "one-room" house, built in concrete block with painted, horizontal board-and-batten. A balcony outside the sleeping quarters overlooks the large, two-story living room.

Wright's major non-domestic commission of the inter-war period was the S.C. Johnson Administration

ABOVE: *Carl Post House (Barrington Hills, Illinois, 1956). One of the four prefabricated house designs by Wright for the Marshall Erdman Company. In this example, the walkway between the kitchen and garage was twice as wide as in most of the others.*

ABOVE: *Carl Post House (Barrington Hills, Illinois, 1956). Built to an L-plan, this house has a masonry core and is built of brick with horizontal board-and-batten siding on the bedroom wing.*

INSET: *The term "prefab" belies the quality of construction and the excellent design of these homes, which are of typical Wright standards.*

Building (1936). Like the Larkin Building, it was conceived with the intention of improving the working conditions of the employees. The Johnson Company had become well known for its interest in the welfare of its staff: it had been a pioneer in the introduction of paid holidays, the eight-hour working day and profit-sharing. The design of the Administration Building reused ideas Wright had envisaged using for the construction of a newspaper building, for *The Capital Journal* in Salem, Oregon, which was never built. The most notable "borrowing" was the concrete and steel columns he had designed to support duplex apartments above a huge, two-story high hall. This would have contained the newspaper's printing presses at ground level and glass-encased offices on the mezzanine level overlooking the presses. Wright called the columns "dendriform" or "tree-shaped" - although they are in fact upside-down trees, since the narrowest part of the column is at the

RIGHT: S.C. *Johnson Administration Building (Racine, Wisconsin, 1936). View of the Main Office - the "Great Workroom" - showing Wright's total working environment in its most homogenous form, with its dramatic top-lighting and inward-looking design. The main offices were completed in 1939, and have columns capable of supporting six times the weight imposed on them. The building is of brick and tubular glass, and its completion saw a resurge in Wright's reputation as an architect.*

ABOVE: S.C. Johnson Administration Building (Racine, Wisconsin, 1936). Wright's specially-designed chairs are still in use throughout the building. His confident incorporation of new building methods and materials impressed a new generation of architects.

base and they increase in size to vast, circular "roots," which are joined to other "roots." These circular caps, sometimes described as "lily pads," do not support the roof, but actually are the roof. In the spaces between the columns in the Administration Building, light is admitted through Pyrex glass tubes, while the 128-foot by 208-foot "great workroom" below contains nothing except the office furniture - designed by Wright - that the staff needed to carry out their work. The use of translucent glass tubing instead of transparent window glass was unprecedented and not without problems. While there was no doubt about its beauty and the quality of light it provided, when the sun struck it at an angle it produced a blinding glare. Furthermore, in rainy weather it leaked! Despite numerous attempts to solve the problem, in the end the rooftop tubing was covered over with a second roof and artificial lighting was introduced between this roof and the glass tubing to simulate daylight.

The perimeter walls of the S.C. Johnson Administration Building, freed from any support role, extended the theme of the ceiling design by terminating in an upper band of glass tubes, which ran continuously around the building. The bricks used in both the interior and exterior walls were custom-made in 200 different shapes to produce the required curves and angles of the building's rounded corners. Between the bricks, the horizontal mortar joints were raked to preserve the streamlined effect. Heating was provided by special wrought-iron steam pipes under the concrete floor and the building was fully air-conditioned with vents provided by the cylindrical "nostrils" emerging at roof level. As in the Larkin Building, the central main entrance was not in the street façade. Here, for efficiency, Wright placed the main entrance at the rear, next to the carport. The S.C. Johnson Administration Building successfully combined Wright's beliefs in organic structures and his acknowledgement of the age of the machine.

Although Hib Johnson frequently asserted through the long process of building the Administration Building that he would never again employ Wright on any project, he did commission two other projects - his own house, "Wingspread," and for a second building for the Johnson Company, a research tower.

The S.C. Johnson Company Research Tower (1944) was to provide new quarters for the company's research

RIGHT: *S.C. Johnson Administration Building (Racine, Wisconsin, 1936). The interior corridors of the Administration building have glass walls that are constructed of Pyrex glass tubing, which provides both diffused lighting and insulation.*

and development division. Using a circular yet rectilinear theme, the Research Tower echoes the central support principles of the dendriform columns of the Administration Building. Like a strong tree, the 14-story tower forms a central core from which reinforced concrete slabs are cantilevered to form alternating square floors and circular balconies contained in a skin of brick and glass. A central shaft contains the stairwell, elevator shafts, and the electrical and mechanical systems and the whole tower is linked to the main building by a covered bridge. The additional stories to the east of the tower, based roughly on Wright's plans, were constructed in 1961, and in 1978 two black granite sculptures (representing the figures of Nakoma and Nakomis, that Wright had designed in 1924 for an unexecuted project in Wisconsin) were installed in the Research Tower courtyard.

With the Research Tower, Wright demonstrated that he was no longer confined to horizontal structures and both the Administration Building and the Research Tower brought the geometric form of the circle into

LEFT: S.C. *Johnson Research Tower (Racine, Wisconsin, 1936). The Administration Building and the Research Tower have been designated by the A.I.A. in their list of 17 buildings to be retained as supreme examples of Wright's architectural contribution to American culture.*

Wright's architecture as a positive force for the first time. The discovery of the potential of circular geometry was to inspire Wright to create an entire new vocabulary of architectural forms, which would culminate in the circle-spiral of the Guggenheim Museum in New York.

Between 1938 and 1953, Wright was also working on designs for the campus at Florida Southern College. The project was initiated by the president of the college from 1925 to 1957, Dr. Ludd Myrl Spivey, an ordained Methodist minister and lifelong disciple of the philosopher John Dewey. Despite the fact that his college had little endowment, few wealthy alumni, a not very impressive academic record, and a student body (mostly of girls) who had to finance their own way through college through working, Spivey was determined that his college should prosper - particularly since it had managed to weather the worst years of the Depression.

ABOVE: *Florida Southern College (Lakeland, Florida, 1938-54). The master plan for the campus was designed in 1938, but the individual structures were only built as funds allowed. In the Industrial Arts and the Science and Cosmography buildings, the esplanades linking Wright's buildings form an extension of the outer walls.*

He envisaged a lakeside campus complete with chapel, library, administration building, faculty housing, student dormitories, classrooms, an industrial arts building, and music, science and cosmography buildings - as well as an art gallery with studio-workshop facilities.

Realizing that a building program was the best way of attracting attention, Spivey commenced fund raising activities for a new chapel - an appropriate building since the college's mission remained in part the training of Methodist ministers. In April 1938, Spivey wired Wright in Arizona requesting a conference to discuss his plans for, as he called it, "a great educational temple." Spivey did not mention the fact that he didn't have any money to pay for this temple and, like many of Wright's clients, it came as a great surprise to him that the great architect agreed to undertake the design. Wright, as usual, was strapped for cash but was always optimistic that a fee would materialize. Yet, in this instance the lack of funds did not appear to worry him. Spivey was offering him a major opportunity: to design the master plan for an entire campus, of which the hexagonal Annie Pfeiffer Chapel would be the centerpiece (and the main source of fund-raising). Wright agreed to lay out a plan that would eventually include 18 buildings - of which 10 were actually built. Over the next 20 years, buildings of Wright's design took form. It was a slow process: Spivey would write to Wright complaining of the lateness in the delivery of plans; Wright would respond immediately with apologies and promise their imminent delivery. Wright would complain to Spivey that he and his apprentices at Taliesin were in danger of starving to death if they did not get some money from him soon; Spivey would reply with apologies and nearly always enclose a check.

The tallest building of the complex - and the focal point of the plan - is the hexagonal Annie Pfeiffer Chapel, the strong vertical silhouette of which provides a visual counterpoint to the three low, flat-roofed, rectangular seminar buildings, built in 1940, and the circular reading room of the Roux Library, built in 1941. Pierced blocks in the side walls of the chapel allow light into the auditorium from the side, while from above light falls through the mass of slanting skylights that are supported by a skeletal steel tower. The other Wright-designed buildings on the campus include the Watson Administration Building - actually two buildings separated by a courtyard containing a reflecting pool and connected by a walkway - and the Industrial Arts Building, which has interior courtyards. There is also the Danforth Chapel, and the three-story Science and Cosmography Building, which houses the only planetarium designed by Wright.

PREVIOUS PAGE: *Florida Southern College (Lakeland, Florida, 1938-54). The Annie Pfeiffer Chapel is the tallest of Wright's designs on the campus. Inside it has no altar, and is reminiscent of Wright's auditoria designs - especially with its top lighting.*

LEFT: *Interior of the auditorium. Wright's buildings on the campus are the Annie Pfeiffer Chapel (1938), three Seminar Buildings (1940), the Roux Library (1941), the Industrial Arts Building (1942), the Administration Building (1945), the Water Dome (1948), the Science and Cosmography Building (1953) and the Danforth Chapel (1954).*

FOLLOWING PAGE: *Florida Southern College (Lakeland, Florida, 1938-54). Science and Cosmography Building. Most of the buildings are of "textile-block" textured concrete - often inset with colored glass - brick and steel.*

Once again, Wright's ideas regarding "integrated ornament" are apparent in the contrast of smooth, textured and perforated cast-concrete blocks. Set into the blocks are abstract patterns of colored glass for decorative effect. Extending from the copper-trimmed roofs are trellises, which Wright intended as supports for vines, and the garden metaphor is carried further in the large planters on the flat-roofed walkways, and the orange trees preserved from the original site.

Like Taliesin West, the campus buildings were largely built with the help of unskilled labor provided by the

students of the college themselves. Students earned a portion of their tuition fees by mixing and pouring concrete for the floor slabs, walkways and the tens of thousands of concrete blocks that served as the basic module for the buildings.

As early as 1929, Wright had proposed an apartment block in the form of a vertical structure. In 1952 his idea was built in the form of the Price Tower in Bartlesville, Oklahoma. When Harold C. Price approached Wright with the commission to design a building for his oil pipeline construction firm, he had in mind a two or three-story building with parking for around 10 trucks. Wright rejected the concept as inefficient and several months later presented Price with the drawings for a 19-story, 37,000-square foot multi-use tower, which would function as the corporate headquarters with additional space for apartments and offices. Wright described the tower as "a needle on the prairie" and "a tree escaped from the forest." The design is, in fact, very tree-like, for its concrete floor slabs cantilever like branches from four interior vertical supports of steel-reinforced concrete.

RIGHT: *Price Company Tower (Bartlesville, Oklahoma, 1952). Rising majestically out of the surrounding prairie to a height of 221 feet, this 19-story tower has a gold-tinted glass exterior with copper louvers and copper-faced parapets.*

The building increases substantially in area from floor to floor as the tower rises, rather like the canopy of a tree. Each glass-fronted apartment of office sheds rainwater clear of the floor below. The concrete floor slabs, like branches, are thickest near the supporting shafts and get thinner (to three inches thick) as they "grow" outwards towards the exterior screen walls. The exterior walls are ornamental screens, because they have been freed of their load-bearing function. The outer enclosing screens are made of glass and 20-inch copper louvers, which shade the inner window surfaces of gold-tinted glass.

At 186 feet tall, the Price Tower is made up of a two-story base, and a 17-story tower. The supporting members are located inside the building and carry the elevators. Most of the upper floors contain four diamond-shaped units allocated for use as offices or apartments. Each space is separated from the others as all look outwards: the exterior walls of each apartment and office are entirely of glass set into metal framing. According to Wright, in *The Story of the Tower*, which was published by the Horizon Press in 1956, the building was

LEFT: *Price Company Tower (Bartlesville, Oklahoma, 1952). Detail of the exterior copper louvers. The residential areas are marked by vertical louvers, while those of the working spaces are set horizontally. The tower is constructed of reinforced concrete with cantilevered floors.*

LEFT: *Price Company Tower (Bartlesville, Oklahoma, 1952). One of the office interiors in the upper levels of the tower. As well as all the furnishings, Wright also designed murals for the 17th and 19th floors, using diamond and triangular modules.*

placed so that the sun shone only on one wall at a time and the narrow, upright blades or mullions, which projected nine inches, created shadows on the glass surface as the sun moved and thus cut out extreme glare and heat.

The southwest quadrant is a little different in layout: here there is a separate entrance and elevator to serve the eight, two-story offices. The 19th floor -

not a full quadrant - was reserved for Price's office and a rooftop garden overlooking the city. In addition to designing the mural on the 17th floor, Wright also designed the built-in desk and the special glass mural in Price's office.

Completed at a cost of approximately $2.5 million - at least $1 million more than originally budgeted - the tower was an immediate success and provided a large amount of free publicity for the Price Company. Price himself was obviously happy with it, since he later commissioned Wright to design two family homes, in Phoenix and Bartlesville.

Throughout his career, Wright created numerous designs for theaters. As early as 1915 he worked on an "experimental theater" for Aline Barnsdall, with a cycloramic, elevator stage and minimal separation between actors and audience. In 1931 he designed the "New Theater" for Woodstock, New York and a similar theater in 1949 for Hartford, Connecticut. Wright believed that the new theater should free the stage of

RIGHT: *Anderton Court Center (Beverley Hills, California, 1952). Situated in a fashionable downtown section of Beverly Hills on North Rodeo Drive, the Anderton Court Center is built around a ramp and a distinctive central mast. The shops are on four levels and are accessed via the upward-winding ramp.*

LEFT AND BELOW: *Anderton Court Center (Beverley Hills, California, 1952). The access ramp is built to a diamond-shaped plan and it is a precursor of the Guggenheim Museum to come. The shops are all still occupied - and the center, with its stark lines and whitewashed walls, functions as an elegant and stylish setting for a range of expensive products.*

ABOVE: *Kalita Humphreys Theater (Dallas Theater Center) (Texas, 1955). The theater was finished by Taliesin Architects after Wright's death. The design incorporates modules with 60° and 120° angles, as well as circles, and the circular stage drum contains a 40-foot circular stage. The building is a concrete cantilever construction; the foyer has subsequently been extended and the terrace above it enclosed.*

RIGHT: *The seating and the stage are conceived as a unity, and the radical reshaping of the theatrical space - together with the extensive underground workshop and scenery store - make greater communication and control possible.*

the traditional proscenium arch and join the actors and audience together in a more unified space. However, none of these buildings was ever realized, and the only theater ever completed from Wright's designs was the Kalita Humphreys Theater in Dallas, Texas.

In 1955, when he was approached by the Dallas Theater Center's building committee, Wright proposed adapting his design for the "New Theater" for this project. The structure consists of a cylindrical drum containing a 40-foot circular thrust stage, with a revolving 32-foot center platform. Additional performance space is made available through the use of a fixed apron, side stages, and two balconies flanking the main stage. The eight-inch thick concrete wall of the drum is a cantilevered construction that is supported and anchored to the hillside site by the building's backstage area. The complex also includes dressing rooms on three levels and a spiral ramp that leads to the production workshop areas housed beneath the auditorium. The theater can seat 466 people and was completed after Wright's death under the supervision of Taliesin Architects.

Despite the beauty of some of Wright's other works, it is the Solomon R. Guggenheim Museum that will always be considered the ultimate symbol of Wright's oeuvre, even though it was not his last work. The driving forces behind the idea of the museum were Solomon R. Guggenheim and Hilla Rebay. Guggenheim, who had commissioned the museum in 1943, had become a millionaire from a copper-mining business and had an interest in collecting Old Masters. However, Baroness Hildegarde Rebay von Ehrenweisen, better known as the painter Hilla Rebay, painted a portrait of Guggenheim and introduced him to the works of European non-objective painters: soon he was amassing a collection of works by artists like Chagall, Kandinsky, Klee, Mondrian, Delaunay and Lazlo Moholy-Nagy. Guggenheim was then faced with the problem of where to house his collection. Since many other millionaire patrons and collectors were busy establishing museums of their collections, Guggenheim decided to follow suit and Rebay set about getting the project off the ground. The choice of architect fell naturally on Frank Lloyd Wright, who visited Rebay and Guggenheim in New York and in 1943 signed a contract agreeing to design a museum.

The major problem was finding a suitable site - which took 13 years. Eventually one of two parcels of land facing fifth Avenue was purchased, giving the museum the entire block front except for a house on the corner of 89th Street. In the meantime, Wright was busy designing the gradually opening, cast concrete, upside-down spiral "ziggurat." The design is purely sculptural:

here there are no surface embellishments and the streamlined exterior sets the pattern of wall and spaces that correspond to the changes in level in the interior. Inside the main gallery a cantilevered ramp, a quarter of a mile long, curves round the inside of the building as it rises 75 feet to the roof. For Wright, the spiral was the most exciting architectural form because it existed in three dimensions and because the expanding spiral - as in the Guggenheim Museum - seemed to defy gravity.

Works of art in the museum are displayed on the ground floor and in 74 circular bays which line the walls of the ramp. Flooding the building with natural light is a 12-sided, "spider-web" patterned, domed skylight. The design and construction of the museum required more than 700 drawings and numerous sets of construction documents, as Wright battled with city authorities over building codes. In addition to the main gallery there is a smaller adjoining circular structure originally housing administrative offices, but now an exhibition space, a lower level auditorium that seats 300 people, and an

RIGHT: *Guggenheim Museum (New York, New York, 1956). The great spiral ramp takes the visitor five complete turns from top to bottom and the building is flooded with daylight through a vast, central glass dome. The difficulty of handling large works of art in the display area does not lessen the building's dramatic impact.*

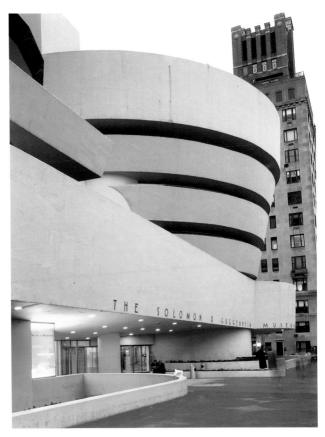

THE SOLOMON R GUGGENHEIM MUSEUM

annex that was completed in 1968 by Wes Peters. The Solomon R. Guggenheim Museum opened in 1959, so neither Guggenheim himself, who died in 1949, nor Wright, who died earlier in 1959, were to see the completed building.

Always a great fan of automobiles and the owner of several, Wright first began working on the design for a prefabricated gasoline station in the 1920s. The Phillips Petroleum Company commissioned him to design a service station and the Lindholm Service Station (1956) in the Minnesota town of Cloquet is a variation on Wright's prototype design. When opened, the gas station

LEFT: *Guggenheim Museum (New York, New York, 1956). The main gallery has a continuous, spiralling concrete ramp. Wright envisaged visitors taking the elevator to the top of the spiral, then walking down the ramp to the ground floor. However, many artists loathed the way that their work was displayed against the sloping, off-white walls.*

RIGHT: *Lindholm Service Station (Cloquet, Minnesota, 1956). Wright's only built service station was designed for the Phillips Petroleum Company - even after Wright had insulted their architectural integrity by disparaging their office buildings in comparison to the nearby Price Tower.*

attracted a great deal of attention and customers - the pump sales set a new record for Phillips 66. Still open for business today on Route 33 and Cloquet Avenue, the design includes a 60-foot illuminated rooftop pylon and an upper level observation lounge, while the 32-foot cantilevered copper canopy was originally designed to hold overhead hoses, eliminating the need for pump islands. However, this part of the design had to be abandoned, due to fire regulations.

Although it is the only Wright-designed station to be built, details such as the V-shaped canopy and the canted windows were incorporated into other Phillips Petroleum stations.

ABOVE: *Lindholm Service Station (Cloquet, Minnesota, 1956). The service station is constructed from painted cement block, with a metal roof and a cantilevered canopy. Details such as the V-shaped canopy and canted windows were later incorporated into other Phillips stations.*

ABOVE: *Marin County Civic Center (San Raphael, California, 1957). This complex includes offices, libraries and spaces for social activities and Wright was working on the plans when he died. It was finished in 1962, and is the closest he got to his dream of building a utopian city.*

FOLLOWING PAGE: *The Administration Building and Hall of Justice bridge the valleys between the three adjacent hills of the site. The pylon was intended to be a radio mast. The design of the building exemplifies how innovative and forward-looking Wright's ideas were - even in his nineties.*

395

When the Marin County Board of Supervisors bought 140 acres of land to the north of San Raphael in California, Wright was commissioned to develop a master plan for the site, to accommodate the 13 local government offices scattered throughout the region. He presented a design for a 584-foot long Administration Building and an 880-foot long Hall of Justice that would bridge the valleys

LEFT: *Marin County Civic Center (San Raphael, California, 1957). Originally the central atriums were to be open to the sky, but after Wright's death practical considerations led to them being covered with barrel-vaulted skylights. The Administration Building is 584 feet long and the Hall of Justice is 880 feet long.*

INSET: *The Post Office on the Marin County Civic Center site is an almost completely circular structure of exposed concrete block, and was Wright's only commission for a U.S. government facility.*

PREVIOUS PAGE: *Marin County Civic Center (San Raphael, California, 1957). The Veteran's Memorial Auditorium which was completed by Taliesin Architects after Wright's death. Its design echoes details of the neighboring Civic Center, expecially in its curvilinear forms and roof design.*

between the three adjacent hills of the site. The focal point of the plan was a low dome, 80 feet in diameter and crowned by a 172-foot golden tower - which housed the chimney. Built out of pre-cast and pre-stressed concrete and steel, the construction technique made use of segmentation and expansion joints, so that the building would withstand significant seismic shocks - the region lies on the famous San Andreas Fault. Originally the central atriums were to be open to the sky, but after Wright's death, practical considerations led to this scheme being replaced by barrel-vaulted skylights. Construction had just begun when Wright died: Wes Peters of Taliesin Architects and Aaron Green, a Wright associate, took over the direction of the project.

The exterior screen walls are divided into arcades and circular openings, which from the inside frame the views of the surrounding countryside. The circular motif is continued in the decorative grillwork and in the gold-anodized aluminium spheres that run round the edge of the roof. As well as offices, the Administration Building is home to the domed, circular county library and the

Anne T. Kent California History Room. The Hall of Justice, completed in 1969, contains circular courtrooms, offices, a restaurant, and the county jail. The Civic Center site also includes a circular post office, Wright's only commission for a U.S. Government facility. As a whole, Marin County Civic Center can be seen as a direct expression of Wright's view that in a democracy it is the citizen and his activities that count. The interior atriums are public and the auditorium, library, exhibition hall, fairground pavilion and pleasure lagoon reinforce the sense that this is a citizen's "civic" center rather than a cold, faceless bureaucratic organization of buildings.

The only civic commission that Wright received from the state of Arizona, where he had lived during the winter months at Taliesin West since 1937, came during the last year of his life: a circular 3,000-seat center for the performing arts. The building was commissioned by Grady Gammage, Arizona State University's ninth president and long-term friend of Wright. It was to be sited on the southwest corner of the campus, originally the site of the women's athletic field. An arcade of 50 columns, 55 feet tall, circles the façade and supports the thin shell of the concrete roof. The plan of the auditorium building is actually composed of two circles of unequal size: the larger circle contains the promenades, lobbies and audience hall; the smaller

RIGHT: *Grady Gammage Memorial Auditorium (Tempe, Arizona, 1959). Wright's last non-residential design to be built, this building is part of the Arizona State University. It has a circular arcade of 50 tall concrete columns supporting the outer roof, and the exterior walls are made of brick and a marble-like composition called marblecrete. A pedestrian bridge takes the audience from the parking lot to the auditorium.*

FOLLOWING PAGE: *The circular 3,000-seat center has a concert hall, theater, teaching spaces and offices. The columns are 55 feet high and the circular shapes of the arches are repeated in the decorative lighting supports along the pedestrian walkways from the parking lot and sunken lawns.*

houses the dressing rooms, workshops, teaching areas and offices, as well as the auditorium stage. The 140-

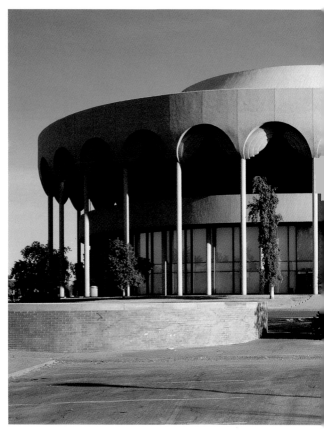

LEFT: *Grady Gammage Memorial Auditorium (Tempe, Arizona, 1959). The extensive foyer of the building allows the audience to move to their seats through 24 doors along the sides and rear of the main auditorium in the European style, rather than along radiating aisles.*

foot wide stage and steel acoustic shell can be mechanically adjusted to accommodate the sounds of a full orchestra and accompanying choir, or collapsed and stored against the rear wall during theatrical presentations. The seating arrangement follows the European style and does not have radiating aisles. Instead, the audience moves to their seats through 24 doors along the sides and rear of the auditorium. Additional seating is provided by a balcony and grand tier, supported by a 145-foot long girder that is not attached to the rear wall of the auditorium and so allows sound to encircle the audience. Two 200-foot long pedestrian bridges - lit by translucent glass globes suspended from metal circles topping overlapping semicircular arches - give access to the building from the adjacent lawn and sunken parking lot. Neither Gammage nor Wright lived long enough to see the building finally completed in 1964. Once again, Wes Peters of Taliesin Architects was largely responsible for overseeing the construction, the engineering and much of the interior design.

THE LEGACY

■ ■ ■

"The architect must be a prophet... a prophet in the true sense of the term... if he can't see at least ten years ahead don't call him an architect."

■ ■ ■

That Frank Lloyd Wright is highly regarded as one of the greatest architects of the 20th century is undeniable: he has left us with hundreds of completed works and thousands of pages of documents covering all of his years in practice as an architect. With a lifespan that extended nearly 100 years, Wright was witness to an age of change: the move into the machine age. It was a period in which a new style of architecture emerged, but few displayed a greater creativity or inventiveness nor contributed more to its development than Frank Lloyd Wright himself.

Wright's importance to the history of architecture in general, and to American architecture in particular, in many ways rests on his introduction of a sophisticated

LEFT: *Carl Schultz House (St Joseph, Michigan, 1957). This house was completed by Taliesin Architects after Frank Lloyd Wright's death. As in most of Wright's other domestic projects, the fireplace forms a dramatic feature in the living room.*

method of composition - all rooms and spaces in his buildings were linked by means of a geometrical arrangement that differed from any other previously used by any other architect. Wright was one of the first

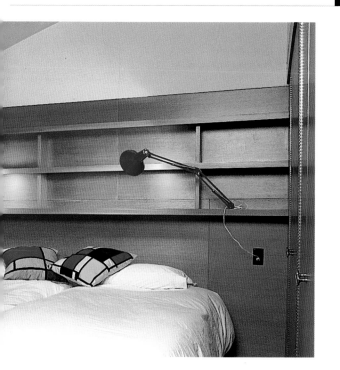

ABOVE: *Carl Schultz House (St Joseph, Michigan, 1957). In one of the bedrooms, extensive woodwork creates a warm atmosphere and even today looks stylish and modern. From the terrace of the house there is a dramatic view of a ravine off the bank of the St. Joseph River.*

American architects to provide a viable alternative to the eclecticism in architecture that prevailed at the end of the 19th and the beginning of the 20th centuries. While many of his European contemporaries - Charles Rennie Mackintosh (1868-1928), Antonio Gaudi (1852-1926) or Victor Horta ((1861-1947) - were working in the curvilinear or rectilinear modes of the Art Nouveau, Wright was building his first houses that destroyed the idea of the house as a large box containing a number of smaller boxes and was introducing the idea of interpenetrating and

RIGHT: *Carl Schultz House (St Joseph, Michigan, 1957). The exterior uses bricks taken from the owner's other properties in the area. The house is a long, low building and has a massive cantilevered terrace and a large basement.*

continuous space.

Wright had a singular advantage over his European contemporaries in the fact that he was born in the United States. This gave him the opportunity first, to assimilate the great traditions of European art and architecture, second, to be skeptical of those traditions when they were transplanted to the New World, and third to reject them. He was no doubt aided in this by his lack of *Beaux Arts* training, which was the usual course for potential architects, but also by the absence of any true "formal" training in architecture. Wright's ability to see the importance of materials in architecture and his spatial awareness were to form the basis of his theory of an organic architecture, in which spatial continuity and consistency was sought in the relationship of parts to the whole. Wright wanted the interiors of his buildings to be considered precisely in terms of their function and, as such, expressed on the exteriors, so that interior and exterior became one.

Wright turned his attention to writing and teaching between 1925 and 1935, and founded the Taliesin Fellowship in 1932. At Taliesin West, the Fellowship program still continues, but it is also the international headquarters of the Frank Lloyd Wright Foundation, which owns and manages Taliesin at Spring Green, the Frank Lloyd Wright School of architecture, Taliesin

Architects, and the Frank Lloyd Wright Archive. The Archive contains 22,000 original drawings and nearly half a million other items relating to Wright's life and works. Taliesin Architects is a professional practice that is the successor to Wright's architecture and design firm. It is based in the old Hillside School, which was remodeled in the 1930s for the Taliesin Fellowship. The restaurant that Wright designed in 1953 was finally built in 1967 and is now the visitors' center.

Some owners of Wright buildings have returned to the original plans in order to restore their properties: Mercedes-Benz has occupied the Hoffman Auto Showroom at No. 430 Park Avenue in New York since 1957. In 1981, Mercedes-Benz hired Taliesin Architects to supervise a restoration that included the installation of the previously unexecuted design for a mirrored Mercedes-Benz insignia in the showroom's ceiling. In 1989, the owners of the Meyers Medical Center in Dayton, Ohio constructed the built-in seating and plywood tables that Wright had designed for the waiting area in 1956; in 1994 the new owners of the Herman T. Fasbender Medical Clinic in Hastings, Minnesota replaced the sheet metal roof with a copper roof according to Wright's original specifications.

The untimely death of commissioner Seth Petersen in 1960 left his property near Lake Delton, Wisconsin

ABOVE AND RIGHT: *Hoffman Auto Showroom (New York, New York, 1954). Here the main display floor is encircled with a concrete ramp. Some of the interior walls are surfaced with glass, as are the structural uprights of the skyscraper that houses this ground floor showroom. In 1981, Mercedes-Benz hired Taliesin Architects to supervise restoration, which included the installation of the previously unexecuted mirrored Mercedes-Benz insignia in the ceiling.*

ABOVE: *Fasbender Medical Clinic (Hastings, Minnesota, 1957). This one-story building is constructed from brick, with a metal roof. In 1994, the new owners replaced the sheet metal roof with a copper one, as per Wright's original specifications.*

FOLLOWING PAGE: *Seth Petersen Cottage (Lake Delton, Wisconsin, 1958). This one-room cottage is a duplicate of the Lovness House, and has stunning views over the lake. It was fully restored in 1989 and is now available to rent as a vacation home.*

unfinished and unoccupied. The 880-square foot cottage located near Mirror Lake State Park was sold, completed and privately owned until 1966, when it was purchased by the state for park expansion, after which a period of prolonged neglect reduced it to near ruin. In 1989, an extensive restoration program returned the cottage to its former glory. Dividing the main living and dining area from the small kitchen is the central fireplace. Both the exterior and interior walls are of locally quarried

421

sandstone and the floors are radiantly heated flagstones. Windows to the south, east and west open up the small interior into the surrounding woodlands and provide a view over Mirror Lake. The furnishings

ABOVE: *Seth Petersen Cottage (Lake Delton, Wisconsin, 1958). Built to a square plan, the cottage is constructed of red sandstone from Rock Springs, near the building site, and finished with mahogany plywood panels and boards.*

RIGHT: *First Christian Church (Phoenix, Arizona, 1950). The First Christian Church - built after Wright's death - was based on an unexecuted 1950 design for the Southwest Christian Seminary.*

inside the cottage were built from Wright's designs and include one of his famous long, built-in settees. Now available for vacation rentals, the Seth Petersen Cottage demonstrates Wright's skills at designing the most modest of living spaces and provides an opportunity for many people to live in a Wright house - even if it is only for a short time.

Testament to Wright's fame, continuing importance and popularity is the fact that, even after his death, his designs - primarily those genuinely planned by Wright,

Above: First Christian Church (Phoenix, Arizona, 1950). The chapel features a stained glass window by a member of the Taliesin Fellowship. The spire has colored glass inserts, through which light floods onto the floor of the diamond-shaped sanctuary.

but for some reason never actually carried out - continue to be built. While most other architects' blueprints and plans lie rolled and forgotten - even during their lifetime - Wright, as usual, is the exception and several of his designs have been completed since his death. For example, in 1972, 13 years after Wright's death, the First Christian Church was completed in Phoenix, Arizona. The church sanctuary had originally been designed by Wright in 1950 as a university chapel for the Southwest Christian Seminary, as one of the buildings on a proposed 80-acre campus. The university never went ahead, but in 1970 members of the congregation approached the Frank Lloyd Wright Foundation with the idea of constructing the 1950 design for their church. The building is supported on 23 triangular steel and concrete pillars, while a narrower range of triangular columns, which frame the clerestory windows, are crowned by a pyramidal roof and a 77-foot spire. Light filters through colored glass inserts in the spire and falls onto the floor of the diamond-shaped sanctuary, which is large enough to seat 1,000 worshippers. The 120-foot, free-standing bell tower has four unequal sides, but appears triangular.

In 1957, Wright had been commissioned to design classroom, office and laboratory space for Wichita State University's Teacher's College. Although preliminary plans were complete by 1958, lack of funding delayed actual construction until 1963, and then only one of two intended buildings was completed - the Harry F. Corbin Educational Center. The two-story, concrete and steel wings of the building - separated by an esplanade, reflecting pool and fountain - are supported by 200 pylons sunk deep in the unstable clay ground of the site. The exterior features large expanses of polished glass, red brick laid with matching mortar, and natural-colored, aluminium, arched tracery. A light tower extends through the opening in the canopy. Inside the custom furniture and woodwork are of solid, red oak.

The Hilary and Joe Feldman House was a Wright house built "from beyond the grave." From the unbuilt

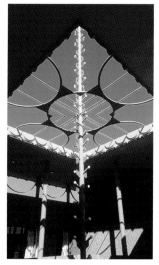

ABOVE AND LEFT: *Juvenile Cultural Study Center (Wichita, Kansas, 1957). Known as the Corbin Educational Center after Harry F. Corbin, who was president of the University of Wichita and the prime mover in getting Wright to design this project, the Center is one of two buildings planned for this site. The second, a laboratory, was never built. The Center has two two-story rectangular units on either side of a patio. Constructed from cast concrete, the building contains classrooms and offices, and has a roof terrace.*

429

projects, the Feldmans chose the plans for the Usonian House that Wright had designed in 1939 for Lewis Bell for a site in west Los Angeles. Nevertheless, the Feldman House seems to fit perfectly in its site in a wooded section of Berkeley, California - despite the fact that Wright himself adopted a site-specific approach to design and that often design changes occurred during construction precisely because of the site. Furthermore, Wright's designs were continuously evolving, so it is not likely that he himself would have constructed a 1939 project at a much later date without changing and adapting it significantly. Several other previously unbuilt designs have also now been constructed.

In 1994, the city of Madison in Wisconsin decided to build a convention center at a cost of $67 million,

LEFT: *Juvenile Cultural Study Center (Wichita, Kansas, 1957). Each unit has an atrium where it meets the central patio, which is enlivened by a fountain and esplanade.*

FOLLOWING PAGE: *Monona Terrace (Madison, Wisconsin, 1938). First planned in 1938 as a building with offices, courtroom, jail and a railroad station, none of the buildings on this site came to fruition until after Wright's death - despite his willingness to constantly revise the plans to suit the commissioners. Although the interiors have been reworked, the exterior of the structure is essentially as Wright designed it.*

utilizing a design that Wright had developed for the same site some 56 years earlier. The plan for Monona Terrace began in 1938 as a city-county building with offices, courtroom, jail and a railroad station. In the 1940s and 1950s the plans went through various developments and changes to re-emerge as

a civic and cultural center, before finally encompassing an auditorium, exhibition hall and community center. Although the interiors of the buildings have been reworked to comply with contemporary city, fire and safety regulations and in accordance with the building's new function, the exterior of the structure and its relationship to the lakeside site are as Wright designed in 1959. The pre-cast concrete and steel building contains a 40,000-square foot exhibition hall, a 15,000-square foot ballroom and banqueting suite, a conference center with seating for over 300, meeting rooms, and a 68,000-square foot rooftop garden.

Inside, in the lobbies and pedestrian promenades, views of Lake Monona are framed by the arches of the

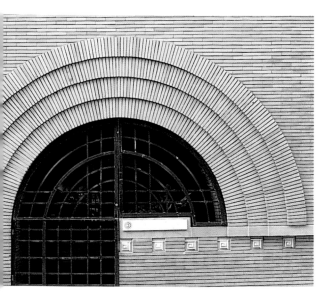

ABOVE: V.C. Morris Gift Shop (San Francisco, California, 1948). Like a Guggenheim in microcosm, this has an interior circular ramp from the entrance to the lower sales area. Its brick façade features a Romanesque splayed portal arch.

INSET: Detail of Frank Lloyd Wright's signature tile that appears on the outside of the Morris Gift Shop. This is also one of the buildings designated to be retained by the A.I.A.

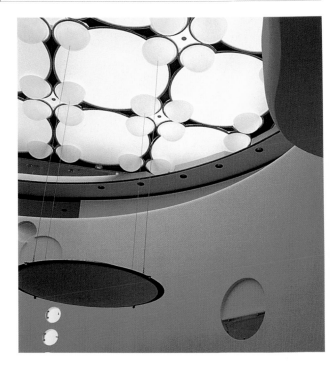

ABOVE: *V.C. Morris Gift Shop (San Francisco, California, 1948).* Inside, the circular form of the Romanesque splayed portal arch is used in lighting and other fixtures and fittings. The building has been used for various purposes, and has been fully renovated.

façade, while outside a curving lakeside plaza supported on concrete pylons driven into the bed of the lake, carries pedestrians and cyclists onto the shoreline park beyond the building. On either side of the building, Wright's favorite three dimensional form, the spiral, is used in two ramps that lead to parking lots.

Even by the time of his death, Frank Lloyd Wright was recognized as the greatest architect that America had produced, and the American Institute of Architects has designated no less than 17 of his buildings as deserving of special recognition. These include all his personal dwellings - his Home and Studio at Oak Park, Taliesin at Spring Green and Taliesin West; domestic commissions - the Winslow House, the Kaufmann House (Fallingwater), the Hanna House (Honeycomb House), the Robie House, the Ward Willits House, the Aline Barnsdall House (Hollyhock House); his public buildings - the Price Tower, the V.C. Morris Gift Shop, the S.C. Johnson Administration Building, the Guggenheim Museum; and religious buildings - the Unity Temple, Unitarian Meeting House and the Beth Sholom Synagogue. Wright's brilliant designs, innovative choice of building materials and practical organization of space have inspired architects all over the world, and there are very few people today who would argue with his own assessment of himself as a "genius."

TIMEFRAME

∎ ∎ ∎

∎ ∎ ∎ 1886
Unity Chapel, Spring Green, Wisconsin

∎ ∎ ∎ 1887
Hillside Home School, Building I, Spring Green, Wisconsin
(converted to Taliesin Fellowship complex in 1932;
demolished in 1950)

∎ ∎ ∎ 1889
Frank Lloyd Wright House, Oak Park, Illinois

∎ ∎ ∎ 1890
James Charnley House, Ocean Springs, Mississippi
W.S. MacHarg House, Chicago, Illinois
Louis H. Sullivan House, Ocean Springs, Mississippi

LEFT: *Warren McArthur House (Chicago, Illinois, 1892). Detail of the panels in the main door, an early example of Wright's fascination with the decorative qualities of glass. The curvilinear, intersecting forms are typical of his early style.*

- - - 1891

James Charnley House, Chicago, Illinois

- - - 1892

Warren McArthur House, Chicago, Illinois
George Blossom House, Chicago, Illinois
W. Irving Clark House, LaGrange, Illinois
Robert Emmond House, LaGrange, Illinois
Thomas Gale House, Oak Park, Illinois
Dr. Allison Harlan House, Chicago, Illinois (demolished)
Robert Parker House, Oak Park, Illinois
Albert Sullivan House, Chicago Illinois (demolished)

- - - 1893

Walter Gale House, Oak Park, Illinois
Robert Lamp Cottage, Madison, Wisconsin (demolished)
Lake Mendota Boathouse, Madison, Wisconsin (demolished)
William H. Winslow House & stables, River Forest, Illinois
Francis Wooley House, Oak Park, Illinois
Frank Lloyd Wright House playroom addition, Oak Park, Illinois

- - - 1894

Frederick Bagley House, Hinsdale, Illinois
Dr. H.W. Bassett House remodelling, Oak Park, Illinois (demolished)
Peter Goan House, LaGrange, Illinois
Roloson Rowhouses, Chicago, Illinois

▪ ▪ ▪ 1895

Francis Apartments, Chicago, Illinois (demolished)
Francisco Terrace Apartments, Chicago, Illinois (demolished)
Nathan G. Moore House, Oak Park, Illinois
Edward C. Waller Apartments, Chicago, Illinois (demolished)
Chauncey Williams House, River Forest, Illinois
H.P. Young House remodeling, Oak Park, Illinois

▪ ▪ ▪ 1896

H.C. Goodrich House, Oak Park, Illinois
Isidore Heller House, Chicago, Illinois
Charles E. Roberts House remodeling & stables, Oak Park,
    Illinois
Romeo and Juliet Windmill Tower, Spring Green, Wisconsin
George Smith House, Oak Park, Illinois

▪ ▪ ▪ 1897

Frank Lloyd Wright House studio addition, Oak Park, Illinois
George W. Furbeck House, Oak Park, Illinois
Henry Wallis Boathouse, Lake Delavan, Wisconsin (demolished)

▪ ▪ ▪ 1898

River Forest Golf Club, River Forest, Illinois (demolished)

▪ ▪ ▪ 1899

Joseph Husser House, Chicago, Illinois (demolished)

Edward C. Waller House remodeling, River Forest, Illinois
(demolished)

■ ■ ■ 1900

William Adams House, Chicago Illinois

Harlan Bradley House, Kankakee, Illinois

Stephen A. Foster Summer Cottage, Chicago. Illinois

Warren Hickox House, Kankakee, Illinois

Fred B. Jones Boathouse, Lake Devalan, Wisconsin

Warren McArthur House remodeling & garage, Chicago,
Illinois

E.H. Pitkin Lodge, Desbarats, Ontario, Canada

Henry Wallis Summer Cottage, Lake Devalan, Wisconsin

■ ■ ■ 1901

E. Arthur Davenport House, River Forest, Illinois

William Fricke House, Oak Park, Illinois

F.B. Henderson House, Elmhurst, Illinois

Fred B. Jones House, Lake Devalan, Wisconsin

River Forest Golf Club additions, River Forest, Illinois
(demolished)

Frank Thomas House, Oak Park, Illinois

Universal Portland Cement Company Exhibition Pavilion,
Buffalo, New York (demolished)

Edward C. Waller Stables, gates & poultry house, River Forest,
Illinois (demolished)

BELOW: *Charles R. Ross House (Lake Delavan, Wisconsin, 1902). Part of the Delavan Lake development, the Ross House is a typical board-and-batten, Prairie-style house built on a T-plan. A second-story extension - which has since been enclosed - converted the plan to a cruciform.*

Henry Wallis Gatehouse, Lake Devalan, Wisconsin

Ward W. Willits House, Highland Park, Illinois

▪ ▪ ▪ 1902

Susan Lawrence Dana House, Springfield, Illinois

George Gerts House, Whitehall, Michigan

Walter Gerts House, Whitehall, Michigan

Arthur Heurtley House, Oak Park, Illinois

Arthur Heurtley House remodeling, Marquette Island,
    Michigan

Hillside Home Building II, Spring Green, Wisconsin

Francis W. Little House I, Peoria, Illinois

William E. Martin House, Oak Park, Illinois

Charles R. Ross House, Lake Devalan, Wisconsin

George W. Spencer House, Lake Devalan, Wisconsin

▪ ▪ ▪ 1903

Abraham Lincoln Center, Chicago, Illinois

George Barton House, Buffalo, New York

Edwin H. Cheney House, Oak Park, Illinois

Fred B. Jones Barn, stables & gatehouse, Lake Devalan,
    Wisconsin

Larkin Company Administration Building, Buffalo, New York
    (demolished)

Scoville Park Fountain, Oak Park, Illinois

J.J. Walser House, Chicago, Illinois

▪ ▪ ▪ 1904

Robert M. Lamp House, Madison, Wisconsin

Darwin D. Martin House & conservatory, Buffalo, New York

Unity Temple, Oak Park, Illinois

Burton J. Westcott House, Springfield, Ohio

▪ ▪ ▪ 1905

Mary M.W. Adams House, Highland Park, Illinois

Charles E. Brown House, Evanston, Illinois

E.A. Cummings Real Estate Office, River Forest, Illinois (demolished)

E-Z Polish Factory, Chicago, Illinois

Mrs. Thomas Gale Summer Cottages, Whitehall, Michigan

W.A. Glasner House, Glencoe, Illinois

Thomas P. Hardy House, Racine, Wisconsin

William R. Heath House, Buffalo, New York

A.P. Johnson House, Lake Devalan, Wisconsin

Lawrence Memorial Library (interior), Springfield, Illinois

Darwin D. Martin Gardener's Cottage, Buffalo, New York

Rookery Building interior remodelling, Chicago, Illinois

First National Bank, Dwight, Illinois

Harvey P. Sutton House, McCook, Nebraska

▪ ▪ ▪ 1906

P.A Beachy House remodeling, Oak Park, Illinois

K.C. DeRhodes House, South Bend, Indiana

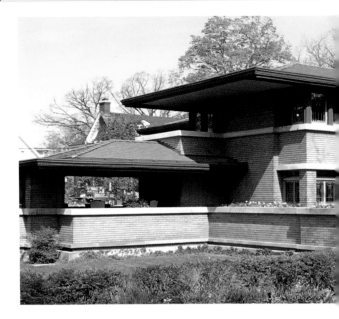

Grace Fuller House, Glencoe, Illinois (demolished)
A.W. Gridley House, Batavia, Illinois
E.R. Hills House, Oak Park Illinois
P.D. Hoyt House, Geneva, Illinois
George Madison Millard House, Highland Park, Illinois
Frederick Nicholas House, Flossmore, Illinois
W.H. Pettit Memorial Chapel, Belvidere, Illinois

ABOVE: *Meyer May House (Grand Rapids, Michigan, 1908). A superb, T-plan, two-story Prairie House, built with Roman brick. Its interior has a great deal of art-glass, and a Niedecken mural. It was restored in 1987-88.*

River Forest Tennis Club, River Forest, Illinois
Frederick C. Robie House, Chicago, Illinois

▪ ▪ ▪ 1907

George Blossom Garage, Chicago, Illinois
Avery Coonley House, Riverside, Illinois
Col George Fabyan House remodelling, Geneva, Illinois
Fox River Country Club remodelling, Geneva, Illinois (demolished)
Stephen M.M. Hunt House, LaGrange, Illinois
Larkin Company Exhibition Pavilion, Jamestown, Virginia
    (demolished)
Pebbles and Balch Shop, Oak Park, Illinois (demolished)
Andrew Porter House "Tan-y-deri," Spring Green, Wisconsin
F.F. Tomek House, Riverside, Illinois

▪ ▪ ▪ 1908

E.E. Boynton House, Rochester, New York
Browne's Bookstore, Chicago, Illinois (demolished)
Walter V. Davidson House, Buffalo, New York
Robert W. Evans House, Chicago, Illinois
Eugene A Gilmore "Airplane House," Madison, Wisconsin
L.K. Horner House, Chicago, Illinois (demolished)
Meyer May House, Grand Rapids, Michigan
Isabel Roberts House, River Forest, Illinois
Dr. G.C. Stockman House, Mason City, Iowa

▪ ▪ ▪ 1909

J.H. Amberg House, Grand Rapids, Michigan
Frank J. Baker House, Wilmette, Illinois

Hiram H. Baldwin House, Kenilworth, Illinois

City National Bank & Hotel, Mason City, Iowa

Como Orchards Summer Colony, Darby, Montana

Bitter Root Inn, Darby, Montana (demolished)

Robert Clark House additions, Peoria, Illinois

Dr. William H. Copeland House remodeling & garage, Oak Park, Illinois

Mrs. Thomas Gale House, Oak Park, Illinois

Kibben Ingalls House, River Forest, Illinois

E.P. Irving House, Decatur, Illinois

Robert Mueller House, Decatur, Illinois

Oscar M. Steffens House, Chicago, Illinois (demolished)

George C. Stewart House, Montecito, California

Stohr Arcade & shops, Chicago, Illinois (demolished)

Thurber's Art Gallery, Chicago, Illinois (demolished)

Edward C. Waller Bathing Pavilion, Charlevoix, Michigan

Rev J.R. Ziegler House, Frankfort, Kentucky

▪ ▪ ▪ 1910

City National Bank & Hotel Law Office remodeling, Mason City, Iowa (demolished)

Universal Portland Cement Company Exhibition Pavilion, Madison Square Garden, New York (demolished)

▪ ▪ ▪ 1911

Taliesin I, Spring Green, Wisconsin (partly demolished)

William F. Kier House (Glencoe, Illinois, 1915). Located in the Ravine Bluffs Development, this square plan house has a hipped roof. Its porch has been modified.

Herbert Angster House, Lake Bluff, Illinois (demolished)
O.B. Balch House, Oak Park, Illinois
Pavilion, Banff National Park, Alberta, Canada (demolished)
Avery Coonley Stables & gardener's cottage, Riverside, Illinois
Lake Geneva Inn, Lake Geneva, Wisconsin (demolished)

▪ ▪ ▪ 1912

Avery Coonley Playhouse, Riverside, Illinois
William B. Greene House, Aurora, Illinois
Francis W. Little House II, Wayzata, Minnesota (demolished)
Park Ridge Country Club remodeling, Park Ridge, Illinois
    (demolished)

▪ ▪ ▪ 1913

Harry S. Adams House, Oak Park, Illinois
Midway Gardens, Chicago, Illinois (demolished)

▪ ▪ ▪ 1914

Taliesin II, Spring Green, Wisconsin (partly demolished)

▪ ▪ ▪ 1915

Emil Bach House, Chicago, Illinois
Sherman Booth House, Glencoe, Illinois
E.D. Brigham House, Glencoe, Illinois
A.D. German Warehouse, Richland Center, Wisconsin
Ravine Bluffs Housing Development, Glencoe, Illinois

▪ ▪ ▪ 1916

Joseph Bagley House, Grand Beach, Michigan
Frederick C. Bogk House, Milwaukee, Wisconsin
W.S. Carr House, Grand Beach, Michigan
Imperial Hotel, Tokyo, Japan (demolished)
Imperial Hotel Annex, Tokyo, Japan
Duplex apartments for Arthur Minkwitz, Milwaukee, Wisconsin
    (demolished)
Duplex apartments for Arthur L. Richards Company,
    Milwaukee, Wisconsin (American System Ready-Cut
    House)
Arthur L. Richards Company Small Houses, Milwaukee, Wisconsin
Ernest Vosburgh House, Grand Beach, Michigan

▪ ▪ ▪ 1917

Henry J. Allen House, Wichita, Kansas
Aline Barnsdall "Hollyhock House," Los Angeles, California
Aisaku Hayashi House, Tokyo, Japan
Stephen M.B. Hunt House, Oshkosh, Wisconsin

▪ ▪ ▪ 1918

Arinobu Fukuhara House, Hakone, Japan (demolished)
Tazaemon Yamamura House, Ashiya, Japan

▪ ▪ ▪ 1920

Aline Barnsdall Residence A, Los Angeles, California

▪ ▪ ▪ 1921

Jiyu Gakuen School of the Free Spirit, Tokyo, Japan
Aline Barnsdall Residence B, Los Angeles, California

▪ ▪ ▪ 1922

Harper Avenue Studio, Los Angeles, California

▪ ▪ ▪ 1923

Charles Ennis House, Los Angeles, California
Samuel Freeman House, Los Angeles, California
Alice Millard House "La Miniatura," Pasadena, California
Nathan C. Moore House rebuilding, Oak Park, Illinois
John Storer House, Los Angeles, California

▪ ▪ ▪ 1924

Indian Figure Sculptures (designed for another building but
    installed in the courtyard of the S.C. Johnson Research
    Tower, Racine, Wisconsin in 1978)

▪ ▪ ▪ 1925

Taliesin III, Spring Green, Wisconsin

▪ ▪ ▪ 1927

Arizona Biltmore Hotel (with Albert McArthur), Phoenix,
    Arizona
Darwin D. Martin "Greycliff House," Derby, New York

Ras-el-Bar Beach Cottages, Damyat, Egypt (demolished)

▪ ▪ ▪ 1928
Ocatillo, Chandler, Arizona (Wright's temporary southwestern headquarters)

▪ ▪ ▪ 1929
Chandler Land Improvement Camp Cabins, Chandler, Arizona (demolished)
Richard Lloyd Jones House, Tulsa, Oklahoma

▪ ▪ ▪ 1932
Taliesin Fellowship Complex, Spring Green, Wisconsin (conversion of existing Hillside Home School)

LEFT: Hollis R. Root House (Glencoe, Illinois, 1915). Located in the Ravine Bluffs Development, the Root House is very similar to the nearby Perry House. It had been badly neglected and fallen into disrepair, but was sympathetically restored in the 1980s.

ABOVE: Lute F. Kissam House (Glencoe, Illinois, 1915). Located in the Ravine Bluffs Development, the main plan of this house is a square, but it has an open porch attached.

▪ ▪ ▪ 1933

Hillside Playhouse, Spring Green, Wisconsin

Malcolm Willey House, Minneapolis, Minnesota

▪ ▪ ▪ 1935

Edgar J. Kaufmann House "Fallingwater," Bear Run, Pennsylvania

▪ ▪ ▪ 1936

Paul R. & Jean Hanna "Honeycomb House," Stanford, California

Herbert Jacobs House I, Madison, Wisconsin

S.C. Johnson Wax Company Administration Building, Racine, Wisconsin

Mrs. Abby Beecher Roberts "Deertrack House," Marquette, Michigan

▪ ▪ ▪ 1937

Herbert F. Johnson House "Wingspread," Racine, Wisconsin

Edgar J. Kaufmann Snr Offices, Pittsburgh, Pennsylvania

Ben Rebhuhn House, Great Neck, Long Island, New York

Taliesin West, Scottsdale, Arizona

▪ ▪ ▪ 1938

Project for Monona Terrace, Madison, Wisconsin (finally built in 1994 after being updated by Taliesin Architects to meet modern Building and Fire Regulations)

Master plan for Florida Southern College, Lakeland, Florida

Annie Pfeiffer Chapel, Florida Southern College, Lakeland, Florida

Project for Ralph Jester All-plywood House, Palos Verdes, California, (finally built in 1971 at Taliesin West, Scottsdale, Arizona by Bruce Brooks Pfeiffer, Director of Archives at the Frank Lloyd Foundation)

Edgar J. Kaufmann Guesthouse, Bear Run, Pennsylvania

Charles Manson House, Wausau, Wisconsin

Midway Farm Buildings, Spring Green, Wisconsin

Sun Top Homes (quadruple house), Ardmore, Pennsylvania

▪ ▪ ▪ 1939

Project for L.N. Bell, Los Angeles, California (finally built in 1974 as the Joe Feldman House, Berkeley, California)

Andrew F. Armstrong House, Ogden Dunes, Indiana

Sidney Bazett House, Hillsborough, California

Joseph Euchtman House, Baltimore, Maryland

Lloyd Lewis House, Libertyville, Illinois

Rose & Gertrude Pauson House, Phoenix, Arizona

John C. Pew House, Madison, Wisconsin

Loren Pope House, Falls Church, Virginia (moved from Falls Church to Mount Vernon in 1964 to make way for a new interstate highway)

Stanley Rosenbaum House, Florence, Alabama

Bernard Schwartz House, Two Rivers, Wisconsin

Auldbrass Plantation, Yemassee, South Carolina
George Sturges House "Skyeway," Brentwood Heights,
    Los Angeles, California
Alma Goetsch & Kathrine Winkler House, Okemos, Michigan

- - - 1940
Gregor Affleck House, Bloomfield Hills, Michigan
Theodore Baird House, Amherst, Massachusetts
James Christie House, Bernardsville, New Jersey
Community Church, Kansas City, Missouri
Seminar Buildings, Florida Southern College, Lakeland, Florida
Arch Oboler Gatehouse, Malibu, California
Clarence Sondern House, Kansas City, Missouri

- - - 1941
Roux Library, Florida Southern College, Lakeland, Florida
Arch Oboler Retreat, Malibu, California
Stuart Richardson House, Glen Ridge, New Jersey
Carlton D. Wall "Snowflake House," Detroit, Michigan

- - - 1942
Industrial Arts Building, Florida Southern College, Lakeland,
    Florida

- - - 1943
Lloyd Lewis Farm Unit, Libertyville, Illinois

ABOVE: *Albert Adelman House (Fox Point, Wisconsin, 1948). Wright designed a laundry for Adelman in 1945, but the project did not go ahead. However, the house he designed three years later was built. It is a long, low in-line building on an 1-plan, with the garage offset to the north and accessed by a covered walkway. Wright also designed a house in 1951 for Adelman's father, Benjamin, in Arizona.*

RIGHT: *View of the main living area, with its high, wood-beamed ceiling. The house is set with its back to woodland, but overlooks a patio and grassy lawn.*

▪ ▪ ▪ 1944

Herbert Jacobs House II (solar hemicycle), Middleton,
   Wisconsin

S.C. Johnson Wax Company Research Tower, Racine, Wisconsin

▪ ▪ ▪ 1945

Administration Building, Florida Southern College, Lakeland,
   Florida

Arnold Friedman Lodge, Pecos, New Mexico

Lowell Walter House, Quasqueton, Iowa

Taliesin Dams, Spring Green, Wisconsin

▪ ▪ ▪ 1946

Amy Alpaugh House, Northport, Michigan

Esplanades, Florida Southern College, Lakeland, Florida

Douglas Grant House, Cedar Rapids, Iowa

Chauncey Griggs House, Tacoma, Washington

Dr. Alvin Miller House, Charles City, Iowa

Melvyn Maxwell Smith House, Bloomfield Hills, Michigan

Unitarian Meeting House, Shorewood Hills, Wisconsin

▪ ▪ ▪ 1947

Dr. A.H. Bulbulian House, Rochester, Minnesota

Dairy & Machine Shed, Midway Barns, Spring Green, Wisconsin

Master plan for Galesburg Village Housing and Parkwyn Village
   Housing,

Kalamazoo, Michigan
Master plan for Usonia II Housing, Pleasantville, New York

▪ ▪ ▪ 1948

Albert Adelman House, Fox Point, Wisconsin
Carroll Alsop House, Oskaloosa, Iowa
Additions to Sondern House for Arnold Adler, Kansas City, Missouri
Erling Brauner House, Okemos, Michigan
Maynard Buehler House, Orinda, California
Samuel Eppstein House, Galesburg Village, Kalamazoo, Michigan
Water Dome, Florida Southern College, Lakeland, Florida
Sol Friedman House, Usonia II, Pleasantville, New York
Willis Hughes House "Fountainhead," Jackson, Mississippi
Edgar J. Kaufmann Guesthouse additions, Bear Run, Pennsylvania
Herman T. Mossberg House, South Bend, Indiana
Jack Lamberson House, Oskaloosa, Iowa
Robert Levin House, Parkwyn Village, Kalamazoo, Michigan
Curtis Meyer House, Galesburg Village, Kalamazoo, Michigan
V.C. Morris Gift Shop, San Francisco, California
Eric Pratt House, Galesburg Village, Kalamazoo, Michigan
Stanley Rosenbaum House additions, Florence, Alabama
Lowell Walter Boathouse and River Pavilion, Quasqueton, Iowa
David Weisblatt House, Galesburg Village, Kalamazoo, Michigan

Charles T. Weltzhiemer House, Oberlin, Ohio

Mrs. Clinton Walker House, Carmel, California

Iovanna Lloyd Wright "Sun Cottage," Taliesin West, Scottsdale, Arizona

▪ ▪ ▪ 1949

Howard Anthony House, Benton Harbor, Michigan

Eric Brown House, Parkwyn Village, Kalamazoo, Michigan

Cabaret-Theater, Taliesin West, Scottsdale, Arizona

James Edwards House, Okemos, Michigan

Kenneth Laurent House, Rockford, Illinois

Ward McCartney House, Parkwyn Village, Kalamazoo, Michigan

Henry J. Neils House, Minneapolis, Minnesota

Edward Serlin House, Usonia II, Pleasantville, New York

▪ ▪ ▪ 1950

Robert Berger House, San Anselmo, California

Raymond Carlson House, Phoenix, Arizona

John O. Carr House, Glenview, Illinois

Dr. Richard Davis House, Marion, Indiana

S.P. Elam House, Austin, Minnesota

RIGHT: *Randall Fawcett House (Los Banos, California, 1955). Designed with two wings, the Fawcett House is constructed from exposed concrete block. The wings are set at 60 degree angles to the main living space, which contains a walk-in fireplace.*

John A. Gillin House, Dallas. Texas

Dr. Ina Harper House, St. Joseph, Michigan

John Haynes House, Fort Wayne, Indiana

Thomas E. Keys House, Rochester, Missouri

Arthur Mathews House, Atherton, California

Robert Muirhead House, Plato Center, Illinois

William Palmer House, Ann Arbor, Michigan

Wilbur Pearce House, Bradbury, California

Don Schaberg House, Okemos, Michigan

Seymour Shavin House, Chattanooga, Tennessee

Richard Smith House, Jefferson, Wisconsin

Project for Southwest Christian Seminary, Peyton Canary, Glendale, Arizona (built in 1973 as First Christian Church, Phoenix, Arizona)

Karl A. Staley House, North Madison, Ohio

J.A. Sweeton House, Cherry Hill, New Jersey

Robert Winn House, Parkwyn Village, Kalamazoo, Michigan

David Wright House, Phoenix, Arizona

Isadore J. Zimmerman House, Manchester, New Hampshire

▪ ▪ ▪ 1951

Benjamin Adelman House (Usonian automatic), Phoenix, Arizona

Gabrielle Austin House, Greenville, South Carolina

A.K. Chadroudi Summer Cottage, Lake Mahopac, New York

W.L. Fuller House, Pass Christian, Mississippi (demolished)

Charles F. Glore House, Lake Forest, Illinois
Patrick Kinney House, Lancaster, Wisconsin
Russell Kraus House, Kirkwood, Missouri
Roland Reisley House, Usonia II, Pleasantville, New York
Dr. Nathan Rubin House, Canton, Ohio
Wetmore Auto Service Station remodeling, Ferndale, Michigan

• • • 1952

Anderton Court Center, Beverley Hills, California
Quentin Blair House, Cody, Wyoming
Ray Brandes House, Issaquah, Washington
Hillside Theater, Spring Green, Wisconsin
George Lewis House, Tallahassee, Florida
R.W. Lindholm House, Cloquet, Minnesota
Luis Marden House, McLean, Virginia
Arthur Pieper House, Paradise Valley, Arizona
H.C. Price Company Tower office and apartment building,
    Bartlesville, Oklahoma
Frank Sander House, Stamford, Connecticut
Archie Teater Studio-Residence, Bliss, Idaho

• • • 1953

Jorgine Boomer Cottage, Phoenix, Arizona
Andrew B. Cooke House, Virginia Beach, Virginia
John Dobkins House, Canton, Ohio
Science & Cosmography Building, Florida Southern College,

ABOVE: *Robert G. Walton House (Modesto, California, 1957). Built of exposed concrete blocks, this house is designed on a T-plan. The rather severe appearance of the concrete shell is softened with a dark wood fascia and trim.*

Lakeland, Florida
Lewis Goddard House, Plymouth, Michigan
Louis Penfield House, Willoughby Hills, Ohio
Harold Price Jnr. House, Bartlesville, Oklahoma
Taliesin West Sign, Taliesin West, Scottsdale, Arizona
Riverview Terrace Restaurant, Spring Green, Wisconsin
Usonian Exhibition House & Pavilion, New York, New York
   (dismantled)
Robert Llewellyn Wright House, Bethesda, Maryland

■ ■ ■ 1954

E. Clark-Arnold House, Columbus, Wisconsin
Bachman-Wilson House, Millstone, New Jersey
Beth Sholom Synagogue, Elkins Park, Pennsylvania
Cedric Boulter House, Cincinnati, Ohio
John E. Christian House, West Lafayette, Indiana
Ellis Feiman House, Canton, Ohio
Danforth Chapel, Florida Southern College, Lakeland, Florida
Louis B. Frederick House, Barrington Hill, Illinois
Dr. Maurice Greenberg House, Dousman, Wisconsin
I.N. Hagan House, Chalkhill, Pennsylvania
Hoffman Auto Showroom, New York, New York
Willard H. Keland House, Racine, Wisconsin
Exhibition Pavilion, Los Angeles, California
Harold Price "Grandma House," Paradise Valley, Arizona
William Thaxton House, Houston, Texas

Gerald Tonkens House, Cincinnati, Ohio

David Wright Guesthouse, Phoenix, Arizona

Hotel Plaza Apartment remodeling "Taliesin East," New York, New York

■ ■ ■ 1955

Dallas "Kalita Humphreys" Theater Center, Dallas, Texas

Randall Fawcett House, Los Banos, California

Max Hoffman House, Rye, New York

Toufic Kalil House, Manchester, New Hampshire

Kundert Medical Clinic, San Louis Obispo, California

Don Lovness House, Stillwater, Minnesota

T.A. Pappas House, St. Louis, Missouri

John Rayward House, New Canaan, Connecticut

Robert H. Sunday House, Marshaltown, Iowa

W.B. Tracy House, Normandy Park, Washington

Dr. Dorothy Turkel House, Detroit, Michigan

■ ■ ■ 1956

Annunciation Greek Orthodox Church, Wauwatosa, Wisconsin

Frank Bott House, Kansas City, Missouri

Allen Friedman House, Bannockburn, Illinois

Solomon R. Guggenheim Museum final scheme, New York, New York

Frank Iber House, Stevens Point, Wisconsin

Arnold Jackson House "Skyview," Beaver Dam, Wisconsin

Lindholm Service Station, Cloquet, Minnesota

Dr. Kenneth Meyers Clinic, Dayton, Ohio

Joseph Mollica House, Bayside, Wisconsin

Carl Post House, Barrington Hills, Illinois

Music Pavilion, Taliesin West, Scottsdale, Arizona

Dudley Spencer House, Brandywine Head, Delaware

Dr. Paul Trier House, Des Moines, Iowa

Eugene Van Tamelen House, Madison, Wisconsin

Wyoming Valley School, Wyoming Valley, Wisconsin

Pre-Fab No. 1 for Marshall Erdman Associates, Madison, Wisconsin

■ ■ ■ 1957

William Boswell House, Cincinnati, Ohio

Herman Fasbender Clinic, Hastings, Minnesota

C.E. Gordon House, Aurora, Oregon

Juvenile Cultural Study Center Building A, University of Wichita, Kansas

Sterling Kinney House, Amarillo, Texas

James McBean House, Rochester, Minnesota

Marin County Civic Center, San Rafael, California (construction through 1966)

Rayward Playhouse, New Canaan, Connecticut

Walter Rudin House, Madison, Wisconsin

Carl Schultz House, St. Joseph, Michigan

Dr. Robert Walton House, Modesto, California

Duey Wright House, Wausau, Wisconsin
Pre-Fab No. 2 for Marshall Erdman Associates, Madison,
Wisconsin

- - - 1958
Dr. George Ablin House, Bakersfield, California
Lockridge, McIntyre and Whalen Clinic, Whitefish, Montana
Don & Virginia Lovness Cottage, Stillwater, Minnesota
Paul Olfelt House, St. Louis Park, Minnesota
Seth Petersen Cottage, Lake Delton, Wisconsin
Pilgrim Congregational Church, Redding, California
John Rayward House additions, New Canaan, Connecticut
Don M. Stromquist House, Bountiful, Utah

- - - 1959
Grady Gammage Memorial Auditorium, Arizona State
University, Tempe, Arizona
Norman Lykes House, Phoenix, Arizona

NOTE: Dates given are those of design, but sources do vary.

RIGHT: *Don Duncan House (Lisle, Illinois, 1957). An example of the
Erdman Pre-Fab I, an L-plan building with a masonry core and painted
horizontal board-and-batten siding on the bedroom wing. The living room
is below the entrance at the intersection of the L, and the kitchen and
dining facilities, with attached carport, are in the short leg.*

FRANK LLOYD WRIGHT